The Blind Man of Hoy

Red Széll

SANDSTONEPRESS
HIGHLAND | SCOTLAND

First published in Great Britain
and the United States of America
Sandstone Press Ltd
Dochcarty Road
Dingwall
Ross-shire
IV15 9UG
Scotland.

www.sandstonepress.com

Editor: Robert Davidson
Photo section: Heather MacPherson
Technical assistance: David Ritchie
Proof: Roger Smith

The publisher acknowledges subsidy from Creative Scotland
towards publication of this volume.

ISBN: 978-1-910124-22-2
ISBNe: 978-1-910124-23-9

Cover design by David Wardle at Bold and Noble
Typeset by Iolaire Typesetting, Newtonmore
Printed and bound by Totem, Poland

To Matthew for faith, forthrightness and friendship

Acknowledgements

None of this would have been possible without a small army of very supportive and selfless people who gave help, encouragement, time, equipment, advice and expertise freely and without much of the grumbling they often received in return from me. Thank you all!

Andres and Cole without whose supreme efforts I would never have made it past the first pitch; and Dan, Isabel, Jimena, Matt and Trevor who, like everyone at Climb London, provided excellent, professional training with boundless patience. I am especially indebted to Paul Ackland of High Sports for giving me free access to all the CL walls. Also Rob and Tom at Mammut for kitting me out for the climb.

Peter, Lee, Cheryl and the many listeners to *In Touch* whose support was so vital in making this adventure more than just a personal undertaking and who, like Steve Bate, reminded me that I am part of a community.

David Head and all at RP Fighting Blindness for running the donations side and being that rare thing, a representative charity in a world of careerist fundraisers.

Omri for designing the webpage and keeping people posted.

Piers, Poh Sim, Al and Anne for wise counsel, delicious tea, poetry and nudging me in the direction of Highgate ponds. And The EGLST (Tom in particular) for persuading me to take the plunge.

Meg Wickes at Triple Echo and Keith Partridge for giving me the best holiday video ever!

Martin and Nick for having confidence in my abilities and for getting me to the summit and back again safely and, like Keith, Matthew and Andres being kind enough to allow me to reproduce their excellent photos.

Bill, Hannah and particularly Dad for braving the first draft of the book. Carl and Tom Bauer for de-chossing the glossary and Alan James at Rockfax for allowing me to reproduce his excellent table explaining the arcana of route grading.

Robert Davidson at Sandstone Press for believing in this story and making it better with his thoughtful editing.

Last but by no means least Kate, Laura and Megan for their unfaltering love and for putting up with my black moods and press-ups at breakfast.

Contents

Acknowledgements   vi
List of Illustrations   xi
Foreword by Sir Chris Bonington   xiii
Fact File   xv

1. Facing Up   1
2. Getting Off   3
3. Formation and Partial Collapse   6
4. Breaking Out of Solitary   12
5. Gearing Up   19
6. The Cole Styron Workout – Part 1   26
7. Al Alvarez   32
8. The Cole Styron Workout – Part 2   40
9. Crack Team   42
10. Seeking Professional Help   60
11. Highland Fling   69
12. The Diff to End all Diffs   81
13. Down to Earth   101
14. Out-of-Touch and In-Touch   111
15. Peak Practice   122
16. Buffing Up   135
17. Day 1, Journey to Hoy   150
18. Day 2, All Talk, No Action   161
19. Day3, First Ascent of the Old Man by a Blind Man   174
20. Day 4, Take Two   199

21. Touchdown 208
22. What Goes Up 215

Appendix A: Glossary of some of the more
   commonly used rock climbing terms 223
Appendix B: Rockfax Climbing Grade Table 233

List of Illustrations

1. Red at Swiss Cottage climbing wall (*photo: Matthew Wootliff*)
2. A guiding hand from Matthew (*photo: Andres Cervantes*)
3. Martin leading off Cioch Nose, note the climbing shoes and the rocky ground! (*photo: Alex Moran*)
4. Route Three, Diabaig (*photo: Martin Moran*)
5. Crack climbing using the elevator door technique at Latheronwheel (*photo: Nick Carter*)
6. Red, Keith, Andres & Martin on the ferry to Stromness (*photo: Matthew Wootliff*)
7. Hoy's dramatic coastline bathed in perfect evening light, from the ferry (*photo: Keith Partridge*)
8. The long walk-in, the Old Man in the distance (*photo: Nick Carter*)
9. Having got him kitted out for the climb, Red's entourage tries to convince him that the Old Man doesn't look so big ... from the promontory (*photo: Keith Partridge*)
10. The long and precipitous descent down the cliff (*photo: Matthew Wootliff*)
11. The route (*photo: Mike Lee, art: Jim Buchanan*)
12. Nick jumaring just above Red (*photo: Martin Moran*)
13. The Crux Pitch (*photo: Keith Partridge*)
14. Nick jumaring just above Red at The Coffin (*photo: Martin Moran*)

15. Red exiting The Coffin (*photo: Keith Partridge*)
16. Keith and Andres filming the climb (*photo: Matthew Wootliff*)
17. It's a long way down and a long way up and it's steep rock all the way (*photo: Keith Partridge*)
18. Approaching the sanctuary of the second belay stance (*photo: Keith Partridge*)
19. A quick rest before the final pitch (*photo: Nick Carter*)
20. Near the summit there's a cleft through the rock as if some giant had taken an axe to the summit (*photo: Keith Partridge*)
21. Rock Gods: Nick, Martin & Red at the summit (*photo: Keith Partridge*)
22. Signing the log book at the summit (*photo: Nick Carter*) Abseiling off – Red and Martin (*photo: Keith Partridge*)
23. Nick abseiling in midair (*photo: Keith Partridge*)
24. Friends reunited (*photo: Nick Carter*)
25. Red during cliff-top interview with Keith (*photo: Keith Partridge*)

Foreword

'After we gave up our attempt on the South West Face of Everest in November 1972, I remember saying to Chris Brasher who had come out to Base Camp to report our story for *The Observer*: "Climbing is all about gambling. It's not about sure things. It's about challenging the impossible. I think we have found that the South West Face of Everest in the post-monsoon period is impossible!" Rash words for, of course, the story of mountaineering has proven time and again that there is no such thing as impossible.'

Those words are taken from the first chapter of a book I wrote as long ago as 1976, *Everest the Hard Way*, after a second attempt with a new team had succeeded in the same 'impossible' mission. On that occasion we put four climbers on the summit, Dougal Haston, Doug Scott, Peter Boardman and Pertemba Sherpa, and possibly a fifth in Mick Burke who did not return. Teamwork had been of the essence as it is on all expeditions.

Ten years before the publication of that book I joined Tom Patey and Rusty Bailie to climb the Old Man of Hoy for the first time, repeating the following year on one of the BBC's first major outside broadcasts. Again, on both occasions, teamwork was of the essence.

These thoughts are prompted by reading Red Széll's vivid and moving account of the first successful ascent of the Old Man of Hoy by a registered blind climber. Before his great achievement many people would have regarded such a feat as impossible. Again though, teamwork was of the essence, and the team that Red put together of professional climbers Martin Moran and Nick Carter, Keith Partridge, who is probably the world's leading adventure cameraman, and Red's two friends Andres Cervantes and Matthew Wootliff, proved to be a sound one. There is a wider team whom the author has properly credited in his Acknowledgements.

History tells us that when the impossible has been achieved it is likely to be repeated in short order. No doubt this will be as true of Red's ascent of the Old Man 'the hard way' as it was after Hillary and Tensing's first ascent of Everest, and it will similarly be repeated. There is something special about being the first though, about being the one who steps forward and says: 'Can't be done? *I'll show ya'!'*

Red's climb, and the excellent book he has written about it, are lyrical and inspiring. They attest to the need for challenge and the value of comradeship. In adversity there is solidarity and behind the dark curtain that Retinitis Pigmentosa has thrown over his eyes there still shines a light. Red climbs because he is a climber as are few people and in that fact lies a mystery which I feel we must let rest. Some can't, some must, but there is no such thing as impossible.

Sir Chris Bonington CVO CBE DL

The Old Man of Hoy Fact File

- It is located off Hoy, second largest of the Orkney Islands, Scotland
- It is a pillar of Old Red Sandstone standing on a plinth of igneous basalt
- It stands 449 feet (137 metres) high
- It was formed by the sea eroding the cliff it was once part of
- Though the rock it's made of is over 500 million years old, the stack itself has stood for less than 400 years.
- The same erosion that formed it could topple it at any time
- It was first climbed in 1966, 13 years after Everest, by (now Sir) Chris Bonington, Tom Patey and Rusty Baillie
- In 1967 an estimated 15 million people watched *The Big Climb*, a live broadcast by the BBC following an elite group of climbers (including Bonington and Patey) as they tackled the Old Man via three different routes.
- Usually the stack is climbed in five sections, or pitches, and descended in three abseils
- The Old Man of Hoy appears both in an episode of Monty Python and in the video to 'Here Comes the Rain Again' by the Eurythmics
- In 2013 Red Széll attempted to become the first blind person to make the climb, the subject of this book

'We see with our brain not with our eyes'
                    – Paul Bach-y-Rita quoted in
    The Brain That Changes Itself by Norman Doidge

1

Facing Up

'The Old Man of Hoy – 450 feet of crumbling sandstone rock rising out of the North Atlantic off the islands of Orkney . . . the most awesome pinnacle in the British Isles.'
                    – Chris Brasher, *The Big Climb*

June 2013

Nothing can prepare you for coming face to face with the Old Man of Hoy.

For months I'd glibly told people that I was going to climb this sea stack roughly the shape and size of the Gherkin. From the top of the promontory it was once the tip of, the Old Man hadn't appeared too intimidating, but with each precarious step down the shattered cliff it had loomed larger, so by the time I was standing on the rockfall causeway that used to form its mighty arch, the giant's stated height looked to be an underestimate.

As a teenager in the mid-1980s I'd watched Chris Bonington and Joe Brown scale this perpendicular monolith in a documentary about *The Big Climb* (the BBC's epic live coverage of their 1967 ascent) and thought, 'I want to do that'.

Within a year I'd found a way to go rock-climbing through school and got hooked.

Aged 19 I'd discovered I was going blind. It was like

1

taking a long fall and wondering whether the person belaying was ever going to stop the rope. After a brief battle I'd hung up my harness for the best part of 20 years and tried to ignore the cravings.

What vision I have left now is like looking into a smoke-filled room through a keyhole – I catch glimpses of parts of things. If they lie at the lower end of the colour spectrum and stay still long enough, I sometimes stand a chance of identifying what they are. The red Orcadian sandstone ahead of me was the colour of dried blood and as unlikely to move. I took it in in stages – a lot of stages.

Martin Moran, the mountain guide who was leading this climb, set off first, the protection (the metal wedges and bolts he'd insert at intervals into cracks in the rock and through which he'd run the rope to catch him should he fall) jangling at his belt like wind chimes. I followed their progress, trying to visualise the line he was taking. After quarter of an hour he stopped and shortly thereafter I felt three tugs on my rope, the signal he was ready for me to follow.

The rock was cold and damp. I explored it with my fingers, testing its slowly decaying strength, before settling on a couple of firm holds. Sea birds wheeled overhead, surfing the light southerly breeze. I took a deep breath, grimaced at Keith the cameraman and stepped up to the first ledge. Only another 444 feet to go. Oh, and the overhanging crux. And all of it being recorded for posterity by TV *and* radio!

If dreams can be planned, this one had got a bit out of hand. My simple wish to emulate Bonington and Brown had gone awry the moment I'd received my diagnosis, but should this attempt at dream-fulfilment turn into a nightmare it would be with national coverage and everlasting documentary proof.

2

Getting Off

'Much of what goes by the name of pleasure is
simply an effort to destroy consciousness.'
— George Orwell

December 2012
It's the week before Christmas and I've just knocked back
my fifth glass of Rioja on top of at least three glasses of
champagne. The hostess is chattering away but my attention
is more focussed on the silk-clad breast pressing insistently
against my forearm. Its owner, one of the mums from my
younger daughter's class, is becoming tipsily affectionate. I
accept another glass from a passing waitress, swig it down
in two gulps and wait for it to numb my sense of dislocation.

I'm not in a good place. Sure the party's great; I'm
among friends, happily married with two delightful
daughters, but inside there's this constant, leaded ache
that poisons my thoughts and refuses to recede.

I knock back another glass and wish that people still
smoked at the parties I get invited to. Oh-oh, bladder
calling. Maybe I should ask the affectionate yummy
mummy to help me downstairs to the loo; who knows
what might happen?

Something snaps and snarls: 'You're beginning to sound
like Joe Wynde and he's such a useless, dysfunctional
prick he can't even nail his second case!'

For the past seven months I've sat staring into space trying to bludgeon the plot of the sequel to my debut crime novel into something worth submitting for publication. Joe Wynde, my protagonist, may share several of my outward characteristics including visual impairment, but his morbid sense of loss allows him to cross lines I only feel comfortable approaching in fiction. Blind as I am, I could never look my wife and daughters in the eye otherwise.

A year and a half ago, when *Blind Trust* had been published, I'd thought at last I'd found a way of harnessing, if not taming, my depression. I'd made it past base camp in the writing world, and with moderately good sales and an audiobook version in my rucksack was well equipped to climb further, but with my new plot tangled and knotted it seems now I'm just left with a longer drop back down.

The waitress has refilled my glass. I lean back into a pillar, away from temptation, and take another swig. Painkiller/ time-killer: I've been doing this with one substance or another for more than half my life, only of late the quantities and frequency have been increasing. It's boring, I'm boring – I'm bored.

I'm in a rut, which as some wag once pointed out, is just an endless coffin. Time to climb out.

A familiar raucous laugh guides me across the room. Swaying slightly I wait for a break in the conversation. All of a sudden I feel good; positive and pain-free; relaxed and ready.

'Evening Mr Szell, you look like you're having a good time.' As ever the ambiguity is there, like a boxer's dance before he gets stuck in.

'Hey, Matthew. Fuck it, I give in. Let's do it. Let's climb the bastard.'

'Really?' That wrong-footed him, though he's still wary. Hardly surprising after my prevarication.

'Yes, really! I want to give it a go – climb the Old Man of Hoy this summer – definitely.'

'Fucking yes! Brilliant! That's great.' And he's slapping me on the back and my glass gets refilled and this time I knock it back in celebration.

'What made you decide to say yes at last?' he asks a few minutes later, after we've explained the commotion to some stunned fellow guests who I suspect think it's the wine talking.

I hesitate. I trust Matthew enough to climb with him, I'm even beginning to consider him a friend but . . . on a need to know basis?

'Oh, you know, I've been mulling it over and you're right, if I don't say yes now we lose another year and then it'll only be more difficult. So yeah, let's do it!'

Someone who did need to know, the decision if not the process by which it had been reached, is my wife Kate. She is somewhat surprised when Matthew informs her.

Shortly thereafter she and I leave the party and a room of people wondering whether my bravado will survive the cold light of day.

3

Formation and Partial Collapse

'Why climb? For the natural experience; for the
danger that draws us ever on; for the feeling of
total freedom; for the monstrous drop beneath
you. It is like a drug'
                                        – Hermann Buhl.

According to my mother I began climbing to escape
boredom and inertia at an early age, learning to scale the
sides of my cot and mastering the downward traverse to
my toy-box before I was a year old.

As I grew up I emulated Spiderman's vertical ascents on
every available play-frame, tree or building and watched
John Noakes' exploits with a mixture of awe and envy.
Blue Peter also introduced me to the great mountaineering
feats of the 1970s and 80s and I followed the expeditions
goggle-eyed on the BBC. The death of Nick Estcourt on
K2 had a greater impact on me than that of Elvis a few
months earlier.

Chris Bonington had become a familiar figure from all
his media work, but it was the simultaneous appearance
of Joe Brown and the Old Man of Hoy on my TV screen
in about 1984 that convinced me I could take my love of
climbing to another level. Bonington was a larger-than-
life gentleman-adventurer type but Brown came across as
an ordinary bloke, a Manchester plumber. And the Old

Man was a rock cathedral summoning the faithful that, in comparison to the mountaineering meccas of Annapurna and Everest, lay on my doorstep.

This form of climbing looked extremely accessible.

Rural Sussex is not renowned for its crags and peaks but the school's Cadet Force promised a summer camp in the Brecon Beacons that included a couple of days rock climbing training with the Army; so I signed up and suffered a year's square-bashing as my fee.

The course was so good that I stayed in the Cadets for another two years by the end of which both my climbing and marching were pretty sound, before escaping to the sixth form rock club with its twice-termly trips to Harrison's Rocks in Kent. I was hooked.

At university I bypassed the Mountaineering Club, my recollection is that they were too Alpine for my taste and pocket, preferring the buttresses, slates and parapets of Cambridge's roofline instead.

The company was good, the protection minimal if there at all. Perhaps it is as well that access to the window ledge necessary to complete *The Senate House Leap* (The K2 of Cambridge Night-Climbing, requiring the traverse of an 8ft wide void 70ft above the cobbles) was barred by the occupancy of a responsible adult in the room beyond.

My nights out on the tiles were numbered anyway. In September 1989, shortly before my 20th birthday, I was somewhat bluntly informed by a consultant ophthalmologist that I was suffering from Retinitis Pigmentosa (RP) and 'could expect to be 'effectively blind by the age of 30'.

RP is a degenerative eye condition that affects the photoreceptors at the back of the eye. First the rods, responsible in the main for night and peripheral vision die off, followed by the cones and their colour vision. If you're lucky the bundle of cells that form the macular and

7

are responsible for central vision hang around for a few years but they too are on borrowed time.

Back in 1989 I was still in the early stages. My field of vision had only decreased by about a quarter of the standard 95 degrees and I had yet to experience the joys of photopsia (the constant kaleidoscope of flashing lights that burst across my vision as my brain tries to fill in the gaps left by my increasingly dead retina).

Climbing, however, is all about trust. If I could no longer trust my own abilities how could I expect anyone else to want to climb with me? At the same time though, more than ever, I needed the release; I needed to feel in balance with myself.

I began to push my luck. Night-climbing in states of Dutch courage that make me cringe for my safety now (bear in mind it was a lack of night-vision that had got me referred to the consultant in the first place) to prove to myself that I could beat the condition.

My favourite ascent, of the North East face of the Fitzwilliam Museum, topped out at a glorious glass cupola where I could enjoy a spliff before my descent. Maybe this is why I can remember so little of the English Literature I was meant to be reading at the time. Certainly being too wasted to be scared stiff saved me from serious injury on the couple of occasions I took nasty, unprotected falls.

Eventually the will to live and a realisation that I was fighting a losing battle grounded me and, if truth be told at least where climbing is concerned, I went into a two decade sulk.

One by one the other sports I enjoyed followed: first cycling, then cross- country and rugby. Substituting them with a rowing machine, swimming and Pilates I continued to keep relatively fit, but these new activities never succeeded in allowing me to vent the frustration I felt at being disabled from pushing myself to my physical limits. And the will to climb smouldered away in the background, reignited regularly by TV documentaries and films like *Touching the Void*.

I'd tried a couple of climbing centres in the 1990s but they had been more focussed on bouldering so didn't satisfy my need to get high at the end of a rope. Consequently when in 2009 my elder daughter announced that she wanted to hold her 9th birthday party at Climb London in Swiss Cottage I wasn't expecting much. How wrong could I have been?

According to a couple of the dads who'd stayed to help, the two South American instructors running the party were 'very tasty.' I too had started drooling on arrival but for another reason entirely. During the 90-minute session I had ample opportunity to check out the 18 purpose-built walls with their multiple routes. They ranged from simple 75 degree 10m-high slabs to a sparsely featured 14.5m overhanging monster. I left feeling my eyes had been opened to a world of new possibilities.

If the staff at Climb London in Swiss Cottage were surprised to receive a new client brandishing a white stick they certainly never expressed it. Rather, as the weeks went by and we got to know each other, they treated it as a challenge that would result in them becoming better teachers and me climbing outdoors again – which of course is where all true climbers should want to be. I was happy to start from scratch; much of the equipment had been updated anyway and two decades of beer and curry weighed heavily on my agility.

Trevor, my first instructor is an old trad climbing hand who works to pay for his crag habit. He worked patiently with me, offering encouragement as I rebuilt my confidence and stamina with a series of Rambo-style assaults on the easier routes, then chatting amiably about great places to climb as I gasped for breath in recovery.

Gradually he began to remind me that by employing skill and technique I could conserve energy and tackle more difficult routes. As the months passed, the prospect of getting out onto rock again became less absurd, until one day as I lay gasping but jubilant having just conquered a tricky overhanging problem and Trevor was waxing lyrical about coastal climbing, I confided my dream of scaling the Old Man of Hoy.

The dream had never died, just gone into suspended animation to be galvanised whenever I saw an advert for the Scottish Tourist Board or watched an episode of *Coast*. Like the summer romance I never quite had with a schoolfriend's older sister, it was cheering to bathe in thoughts of what might have been.

Trevor rubbed his chin and in his calm, considered way said, 'well . . . it's only an HVS . . . with a bit of work you could probably manage it.'

For the next couple of years that was enough. I was content to know that my dream wasn't completely untenable and it remained, a distant goal to work towards. I made slow but pleasing progress, which was a happy counterpoint to my fast degenerating eyesight.

I don't think that I or anyone at home or Climb London really expected me to try to make the dream become reality, but then none of us had anticipated the intervention of Matthew Wootliff.

Matthew had been among the first of the existing parents to introduce themselves when my daughters started school. A sinewy blend of Leeds forthrightness and North West London chutzpah he worked from home and often did the school run. He was also equipped with a voice and laugh that made it easy for me to locate him in the crowd, no matter how close to twilight it was.

In the 13 years I've been one I'm still the only full-time house-husband I've ever met, so it was good to have another dad to talk to; even more so when we turned out to be the only male representatives on the PTA. However, although both pairs of our daughters were in the same forms, neither was best friends. So Matthew and I met mostly briefly, at school functions or in the twice-daily tidal flow through the gates and, like our children, got on well-enough without knowing each other that well.

Over five years I'd got an inkling of the streak of dogged determination in him; enough that when I mentioned I was a regular at the climbing wall and he expressed interest, I was kicking myself even as I suggested he join me.

This was my activity, my time away from my fellow parents and Hampstead neighbours (some of whom were one and the same) – my little bit on the side that I wasn't ready to share . . . let alone with someone as vociferous as Matthew!

Besides he was notoriously fit and healthy, a former ski-instructor who rode a single-speed bike everywhere and whose physique was much commented on by the mums at the school gate. What little physical self-confidence I was regaining by dint of my steady improvement through the climbing grades would be shattered if a novice outstripped my performance at his first or second attempt.

It took barely 70 minutes. By the second route of our second session he was climbing a grade beyond me. His agility was galling. I still beat him on strength and stamina but how long was that going to last? For the first time since I'd started at Swiss I left feeling thoroughly dejected.

That night I seriously considered changing my visits to a day Matthew couldn't manage.

4

Breaking Out of Solitary

'A man wrapped up in himself makes a very
small bundle.'
— Benjamin Franklin

The fact is, by summer 2012 I'd reached a point where I
expected people to make allowances for my disability but
got infuriated when I felt defined by it. I was happy for
my climbing instructors to be amazed that I could tackle
5b grade routes but pissed off when Matthew climbed a
grade higher and they pointed out that he had the advantage of being able to see the holds.

Fortunately the Paralympics came to town and made
me re-examine my attitude.

One of the few joys of carrying a white stick is that so
many people offer help. It might not always be needed
but a gracious 'thank you, I'm fine, but it's always lovely
to be asked' is a small price to pay for feeling the kindness
of strangers.

At the same time it's a bore repeatedly explaining that
'yes, I do have some sight' and 'only 3% of those registered
blind in the UK see nothing at all.' It's hardly surprising
though. In popular culture the blind are invariably sightless; presented either as stricken victims or sonically
super-powered. That's why I'd written *Blind Trust*; to set
the record straight, to educate and entertain, by giving the

reader a behind-the-lens look at what it's like to be robbed of your vision. Building that into a crime novel seemed grimly appropriate.

Of course, I'd been aware that the majority of blind people cite a loss of independence and resultant sense of isolation as the biggest challenge arising from their sight loss, but I'd been confident that my duties as a house-husband would provide a sociable counterbalance to the couple of hours I'd be scribbling while the kids were at school. So it had proved – at first.

The plot had been bubbling away in my head for a few years and poured out easily enough. And though it took a while to find a publisher (a couple even suggested making Joe the stricken subject of a misery memoir or exaggerating his auditory powers), the book had made it to the shelves pretty much unadulterated.

However, what had been liberating swiftly became a bind as I struggled to produce a sequel and discovered that there is no one more isolated or morbidly introspective than an unproductive writer. The authors I'd looked to for inspiration had become monsters, their gigantic talents mocking my puny efforts. Climbing, which had been my weekly reward for good work, became my sanctuary from failure. The last thing I needed was Matthew jauntily cruising up routes I'd taken weeks to conquer, mocking my small steps with his effortless strides.

At the same time I recognised that he too saw his time at the wall as escapism and his untethered, vociferous and often very amusing rants about life cheered me up, in the way that only *schadenfreude* can. After climbing I picked up my kids, but he had to go back to his desk!

I swallowed my pride, bit my tongue and we carried on meeting each Thursday afternoon. After another couple of weeks the work rota at Climb London changed and we were assigned a new instructor. Andres Cervantes, a stocky 26-year-old Colombian PhD student at Brunel, had learned his English while studying Product Design Implementation in Manchester. As a result his smooth South American tones were peppered with flat vowels and visceral slang. Possessing equal measures of swagger and a disarming eagerness to join in whatever was going on, he also proved to be an indomitable problem-solver.

In this respect he and Matthew were kindred spirits and were soon discussing ways of improving communication between me and whichever of them was on the ground directing my progress. Up till then I'd relied on my instructor shouting up my next move, which on the 14.5 metre walls often left both parties hoarse and frustrated, especially since the area behind the sports centre had become a construction site.

Andres' bipolar accent, the fact that he dealt in centimetres while I thought in inches and our mutual inability to know our left from our right only exacerbated the problem. After one particularly bad-tempered exchange that culminated in me kicking the wall so hard I was unable to continue climbing, Matthew insisted we organise a night out to discuss the issues over a few beers.

He challenged us to come up with a system of length and direction that would be simple for Andres to deliver and me to understand. Meanwhile he would investigate two-way radios and headsets so that we could hear each other over the din of jackhammers, angle-grinders and all the traffic that flowed round the Swiss Cottage gyratory.

Matthew and Andres also both tried climbing blindfold, to gain a sense of the challenge facing me.

At another time I might have baulked at their efforts, resenting their interference or finding the blindfold experiment patronising, but my cynicism was tempered by their genuine consideration, then blown away as Paralympic euphoria swept the nation.

Day after day the media was giving extensive and over-whelmingly positive coverage to disabled people. This was no one-size-fits-all portrayal of disability; there were no stricken victims here. The success of these super-fit but otherwise everyday heroes forced you to look beyond their disability and recognise the individual. Medal winners were encouraged to tell their story, and again and again I heard a blend of pride and humility as they expressed thanks to coaches, trainers and support staff. It began to dawn on me that mountains don't get conquered single-handed but by teams. *Blind Trust* had been a solo effort and, in climbing terms, I'd bagged a Munro, but if I wanted to tackle further peaks I'd need to accept the help that was on offer.

So, buoyed by the extraordinary goodwill I was encountering each day on London's streets that summer (which, though muted, persists to this day), I took some positive action, accepted the help on offer and worked with Matthew and Andres to develop a system that would minimise the impact of my blindness on my sport.

Matthew didn't exactly bring a clipboard to the pub but he had made notes and drawn up a strategy. His tart defence was that someone needed to and he'd known I wouldn't. I bought the first of several rounds and he called the meeting to order. He approached the issue of my climbing like the business research analyst I discovered he is. It was an operation that needed streamlining to optimise performance while taking into account certain local idiosyncrasies. He bluntly informed Andres and me that the way we were currently going about things was untenable and more likely to end in strife than success. Both of us were at fault but the responsibility to find a solution lay squarely with me. So how did I propose to make it easier for Andres to give me accurate instructions?

It felt like a dressing down, half-time hairdryer treatment, and put me immediately on the defensive.

'Look, I know I get narky and I'm sorry. But I get frustrated with all the hanging around between moves. I'm wasting all this energy and knackering my arms just trying to hang on while you guys work out what my next move should be. I just want to get on quickly, not hang around in stress positions like I'm in Guantanamo.'

'Yes, and that's exactly what we're here to do – to sort out communication and optimise your outcome on the wall. If you understand exactly what you are being told to do you can conserve that energy for the climb and stop taking your frustration out on Andres and me. So what ideas have you come up with?'

A gulp of beer drew the sting of being addressed like a recalcitrant teenager and I tried not to sound too sulky as I outlined my 'back to basics' plan. I proposed using a clock-face system, whereby if the next hold was above me and slightly to the left Andres would call out 'left hand eleven o'clock'; more than half-left would be ten o'clock. Likewise my feet would operate in the three o'clock to nine o'clock sector, with the centre point of the clock-face being in the area of what Andres referred to as my 'Queen's jewels'.

This didn't fully address the issue of left and right but helped minimise the scope for error (on the climbing wall at least, it's rare to cross your arms). We toyed with the idea of sewing an L and an R to the backside of my trousers but left this as a last resort as it is easier for a fat man to pass through the eye of a needle than for a blind man to thread one.

Distance proved a knottier problem, not only because

of my adherence to imperial measurements that went out of fashion shortly after I was born, but by the difference in perspective between the man on the ground and the ascending climber. Eventually we settled on a system of hand widths from the hold I was gripping to the one I was aiming for.

Neither of these solutions was foolproof but they should, we thought, provide a good and simple basis for getting my hands and feet in the right area. Andres then pointed out that in my impatience to locate the next hold I tended to 'stab in the dark' which meant I often went all around the target; he suggested moving my hands and feet in a widening spiral till I hit what I was seeking – 'also it will make you look more cool on the wall, not like you are in distress' he added. Coming from a suave Colombian bantam this was advice I resolved to take.

Matthew had been looking at walkie-talkies and wanted to know exactly what I needed from a system. Being by far the least technically minded of the three of us I wasn't sure whether what I wanted actually existed but told him it had to provide two-way hands-free communication with a small, single earpiece and mike that left my other ear open to take in what was going on around me. He said he'd have a look at what was on the market. I hoped it wasn't going to prove too expensive.

This led to more beer and further discussion of other tools we could employ. I said I'd try wearing a head torch, to see whether it helped me distinguish between the coloured holds that made up the different routes on the wall (anything from green to violet is just a shade of grey to me), and dig out some tinted glasses I'd once been given which are designed to increase contrast.

As closing time approached and we got chatting about outdoor climbing and places we could go, I was feeling positively buoyant. All this was so much in tune with the Paralympics. Maybe technology could provide me with the visual equivalent of carbon-fibre blades. Who knew what mountains I might yet climb? Then it slipped out. I told them of my dream to climb the Old Man of Hoy and from that moment I became a project.

5

Gearing Up

'Now I approach climbing differently. I have
learned less effort and energy, less obsession,
and more feeling, as with piano, more emphasis
and less frenzy'

— Pat Ament

That night in the pub put the three of us on a different
footing. It kindled the flame of common enthusiasm for an
activity that lies at the heart of so many male friendships –
when we'd discussed climbing weekends away there was
more than beer talking. Also, it had established roles for
us all, which is the secret to all successful teamwork. Each
Thursday, between lunchtime and pick-up, we met at
Swiss to climb, chat and work on streamlining the process
of getting me up the wall.

The clock-face system worked well, though the centre-
point proved to be located at my bellybutton and left
and right remain an issue to this day. Distance too saw
a marked improvement though we soon abandoned the
hand-width measure in favour of educating Andres in
the arcane world of feet and inches. He in turn taught
Matthew and me much of the terminology of climbing
(see *Appendix A*) allowing me especially to adopt correct
positions far more swiftly.

Matthew it turned out had done a bit of climbing before,

which made his rapid progress slightly less galling, and his enthusiasm on the wall was infectious. As the weeks continued Andres began to set challenges for us that made use of both our strengths and weaknesses, some of which we had in common and some of which allowed one of us to shine, so that neither of us felt outstripped by the other. Most weeks Matthew and I would leave our 60-minute session a good 15 minutes late and continue our competitive banter on the walk up to the school gates.

He had also been busy in his allotted task, using his expertise in research to identify a couple of companies to whom he'd outlined our needs. One had come back with a potential solution but this was far from cheap and, having just forked out for a new harness, I was loath to pursue the option until we'd established there was no inexpensive alternative.

So, one Tuesday lunchtime in late September, we met in Camden Town for a bite to eat and a doomed expedition to Maplin's. By now it was taken as read that any equipment we invested in would need not only to be suitable for use indoors at Swiss but also durable enough to survive rough treatment and bad weather on some desolate outdoor crag. Over an excellent burger in Camden Lock he made me go over again, in order of importance, my precise requirements.

The radios needed to be: 1) light; 2) provide two-way hands free communication for both climber and belayer; 3) have a single earpiece that would loop over the ear and stay in place; 4) have a mike that would not get caught in the rope; 5) be durable, shock proof and water resistant; 6) have decent battery life and be easy and fast to recharge; 7) have a good range and more than a couple of channels.

The sales assistant seemed bright and keen enough to help, though I sensed a raising of the eyebrows both at our intended end-use for the radios and Matthew's uncompromising, staccato delivery of our list of demands. But stranger things happen every day in Camden and he equipped us with a system that he assured us should tick all the boxes.

It didn't.

We returned a few days later and reiterated that if the climber, or belayer, had to press a button to transmit then accidents were going to happen. Seemingly we were asking the impossible and we left with a full refund. I felt guilty at having wasted Matthew's time and worried that the whole idea might be an expensive distraction. I tried to communicate my concerns to Matthew but he was on a mission now. He knew that there was a solution out there and he was going to track it down. So my message was not received. Between his fulminations about the incompetence of others, I suspect he was enjoying himself.

In the fortnight following the Camden debacle we considered using mobiles or Skype, only to abandon the ideas on grounds of coverage, cost or potential damage. Piling had started on the building site behind Swiss and Andres was beginning to sound like he'd been gargling broken glass. It was clear that the only way to reduce stress and the risk of voice polyps lay with two-way radio.

Matthew set up a meeting with an expert and if Paul Rawlings was as smart as he dressed I reckoned we were onto a winner. The MD of Paramount Radio Communications wore a well-cut suit when he met us at Islington Business Design Centre, and to each subsequent meeting. He had clearly listened to Matthew's exacting criteria and had brought three different models and various different headsets for us to try.

There was no pressure to buy, just genuine enthusiasm to provide a solution to a project he was clearly delighted to be involved in (I was to discover that he has a friend whose son is not only partially-sighted but has done a bit of indoor climbing). We tested and discussed the merits of each system and opted for a Motorola plugged into a very natty earpiece with a bendy mike bar that was small, close fitting and appeared relatively indestructible. Paul said he'd order us a pair to play with for a couple of weeks then come to Swiss to see how they and we were getting on.

The difference they made was immediate and profound. Although we had a few teething troubles (arising mainly from the sheer volume of background noise causing the microphones to transmit when we didn't want them to, and the difficulty of finding a channel not being used by construction workers or local taxi firms), having Andres' instructions delivered directly into my ear made the vast majority of them instantly intelligible. I climbed more fluently and he, not constantly being shouted at to repeat himself, became more confident in his guidance. Stress levels all round fell significantly as a result.

Something else that made a surprising difference to my confidence was wearing a helmet. After a couple of bruising encounters with overhangs and juggy handholds I sacrificed coolness for common-sense, reasoning that I'd need to wear one outdoors anyway and that it helped keep the earpiece in place.

Over the following month or so Matthew and I made rapid progress so that by December we were both competent on indoor 5c routes – not yet Old Man of Hoy level but heading in the right direction. As with all sport climbing (*ie*, where artificial protection or holds are in-place), a climbing wall is measured in French (F) grades that equate to a lower measure of technical difficulty on the British trad climbing (unprotected) scale (see *Appendix B*). Thus my F5c level at Swiss meant I could expect to climb 4c trad routes, putting only the crux pitch of the Old Man out of my reach.

So why was I still prevaricating and not committing to an attempt on Hoy? Each week Matthew would press me to make a decision. He was keen, Andres was up for it, we'd got the communications sorted and could cobble together much of the other equipment we'd need. If this was my dream, what was my problem?

I'd begun by using the excuse that I needed to finish off my sequel to *Blind Trust,* but as we all knew that had turned to dross weeks before. It wasn't as if the dream glittered any the less for being within reach, quite the opposite.

However, whereas I could be pretty certain that with a bit of work I could achieve the technical grade, I was less confident of making the adjectival grade. This other part of the British trad climbing system gives an overall picture of how hard the whole route is (unlike the technical grade which just rates the hardest move) – how sustained it is, how exposed you can expect to feel.

The Old Man is an E1 not an HVS: – E for Extreme. It was a long, hard, vertical slog, *with* overhangs. And by committing to it I'd be exposing myself to fear of letting others down to some extent and not living up to their belief in me, but more viscerally, fear of not being up to the challenge and having, yet again, to admit defeat of my hopes.

I decided to have a chat with Cole Styron, the Director of Operations at High Sports, the company that owns Climb London. Like many a good trad climber he has a laid-back manner that belies a deep-rooted wild streak. This was perfectly expressed in his possession of both a law degree and a love of extreme sports. We'd got to know each other pretty well over the three years that he'd been based at Swiss and while his straight-talking Oklahoman appraisals of situations and individuals did not always win him favour with his staff, I respected his opinion.

In an email entitled *'an honest question'* I asked:

'In ALL honesty would I be kidding myself and others to even think of attempting the Old Man this August/ September (or at all)?'

His response was encouraging:

Hi Red,

Fucking go for it!

Seriously, however, you'll need to really start training on actual rock, which is very, very different than the plastic stuff in the gym. From the smidgen of research I've done on the Old Man, it seems to be at least in part a crack climb, so you'll definitely need to start working some of that into your training schedule outdoors, as it's not something I can provide you with at Swiss. If you fancy some trips up to the Peak District in the springtime I'm sure we could work that out.

The other issue is of course that the Old Man of Hoy is a trad climb, so there's more to it than just the climbing. You'll need to develop some technical ropework skills, some abseiling experience, and a bit of other general knowledge.

The East Face (which is the classic route) is an E1 5b (which is probably French 6b+ but will feel harder). You'll need at least one partner who leads E2 and up quite solidly. I don't personally fancy it (I'll explain why next time I talk to you in person), but there are people who work for us that might. I can ask around. To be perfectly candid, I don't think either Trevor or Andres would be suitable as your lead guy.

Logistically I think it makes sense for you to climb with

two others. There is no walk off, but instead a series of abseils. You would probably need more guidance coming down than going up (up is always the easy part), so you should probably be the middle man on the descent so that someone goes down first and is waiting at the anchor for when you come down.

We've got some tricky routes at Swiss, up to about 7b+ on the 14m wall. It may be time to orchestrate some proper training, rather than just climbing, into your sessions, but we can talk about this in the new year. I'm done on Wednesday and won't be back until the 2nd, but let's catch up then.

You should quit smoking anyway Red. You've got kids and a wife, all of whom probably want you around for the foreseeable future.

Merry Christmas,
Cole

Of all those who'd watched my progress and knew the challenges of a climb of the magnitude of the Old Man, Cole was the best placed to give an opinion and the least likely to blow hot air up my backside. If he was saying 'go for it' then really I had no excuse. 2014 might be too late; RP isn't a static condition and just when you've come to terms with the level it's reduced you to it has a nasty habit of plunging you deeper into darkness.

Still I prevaricated, until ten days later I found myself necking red wine at that pre-Christmas party and, I suppose, building up my Dutch courage.

6

The Cole Styron Workout – Part 1

'Set definite targets'
– Joe Simpson,
Touching The Void

The 'bit of work' that Trevor had suggested as preparation for the climb turned out to be a full body refurb. I'd envisaged losing a bit of Åweight, doing a few chin-ups and giving up the two or three cigarettes I still smoked most evenings, but Cole had other ideas.

With remarkable serendipity my wife, never a fan of my nightly lung pollution, gave me an electronic cigarette for Christmas. It proved exceedingly effective and filled with an insane zeal for bodily purification I decided to go the whole hog and do what I had for years scoffed at others for doing. I gave up drinking for January.

This seemed to shock more people than my earlier announcement about the climb but it pleased Matthew and Andres as a clear statement of intent. I treated it stoically as the sternest test of my resolve. At least it was until Cole's email turned up a couple of weeks into that dark and gloomy month.

Hi Red
OK, before starting the following training programme, do not lose heart if you aren't seeing progress. Progress

is a slippery thing and comes when you least expect it. I've been working hard for the last six weeks with little effect and getting a little down myself. Then last night I went bouldering and suddenly for no good reason I saw a dramatic improvement. Time and commitment are the main factors, as near as I can tell.

Training Programme

This programme is really based on general climbing fitness and will last for the next four weeks only. After that, we'll change things to a new programme. This first phase is meant to supplement the most important thing you could possibly be doing right now, which is climbing as much as possible.

All four weeks: 3 sessions of climbing (your choice of days) for 90-120 min each week. One session should include 2x20 min of traversing without touching the floor if possible. Bring an iPod! These endurance sessions are really important (as well as really boring) and build capillarity, which is what keeps you on the rock more than anything else. You should also ask Andres to show you some games like silent climbing, and no-handed slab climbing. The next phase will start to get a little more performance-specific and we'll also probably get a shot to go outdoors.

Week 1

Monday, Wednesday, Friday:

After stretching and warming up, do six sets of the following:

One set is:

3 pull-ups (palms facing away, always) then
1 one-arm (each arm one time) hang to failure from the pull-up bar

Rest as long as necessary between sets, but aim to have the whole thing done in under an hour.

Tuesday, Thursday, Saturday:
After stretching and warming up, do six sets of the following:

One set is:
7 push-ups (press-ups?), then
Max crunches (or stop at 30)

Rest as long as necessary between sets, but aim to complete in an hour.

Sunday: Rest

Week 2
Repeat Week 1 workout, but do 4 pull-ups and 10 push-ups. Max crunches stop at 40.

Week 3
Repeat Week 2 workout, but do 7 pull-ups and 15 push-ups. Also, instead of one-arm hangs, on sets 4-6 do one 90-degree lock off and hold until failure. A lock off is where you do a normal pull up, then lower until your arms are bent at a certain angle (e.g. 90 degrees) and hold. If your body starts shaking, you're doing it right.

Week 4
Monday, Wednesday, Friday:
Stretch/Warm up, then start with a few pull-ups (perhaps 5 or so) to get the blood flowing, then give yourself a three minute rest. Then,

3 sets of 10 pull-ups, then a solid rest, then
3 sets of Frenchies with 7 minutes of rest between each set

One Frenchy is a pull-up, lower to 60 degrees, hold for 5 seconds then lower completely, followed by another pull-up, lower to 90 degrees and hold for 5 seconds, then lower, followed immediately by another pull-up, lower to 120 degrees and hold for 5 seconds then lower completely.

Tuesday, Thursday, Saturday:
200 push-ups in as many sets as it takes you (if you can't finish during your workout, finish them later in the day, but get 200)
Max crunches for sets 1-3
2min bicycle crunches for sets 4-6 (check internet if unsure what 'bicycles' are)

Do all this faithfully and at the end of 4 weeks your wife is going to mistake you for the Polish builders you're so fond of in *Blind Trust*, or I'll eat my hat.
    Enjoy,
    Cole

I doubt if anything acts as a sharper spur to weight loss than having to do repeated pull-ups. You curse every ounce as your shaking arms shriek acidulously for mercy and your curled digits threaten to slough off their covering of skin for the relief of letting go the bar above your head. If I'd questioned the wisdom of abstinence beforehand, within two days of starting this boot camp torture I was thanking my stars (and my wife) for the short period of clean living I'd enjoyed in preparation.
    Sometimes hard work is its own reward. By the end of

January I had lost a stone, taking me two-thirds of the way to my target of being 10½ stone (66.6 kg), which I considered the ideal climbing weight for my 175 cm height. I felt more agile, clearer headed and my knees hurt less as I carted laundry, kid's toys and the hoover round the house; and, as Cole had predicted, Kate had noticed the difference.

I still had a long way to go. On a snowy morning in the first week of February Cole met me at the West One wall in Marylebone and, over the course of 90 of the most exhausting minutes I have ever experienced, gave me a masterclass in some of the finer arts of climbing including: flagging – offsetting your weight on one side by extending the opposite one at such an angle that it acts as a counterweight allowing you to stretch further for a handhold; rock-overs – using the same technique to transfer all your weight onto one raised knee then rising up to stand on that leg to bring you to an otherwise unreachable handhold; and locking off – holding oneself in place on the wall with one, or both, arms locked in a bent position, which is very, very tough for more than a few seconds no matter how much weight you've lost. I told myself the cab home was simply a reaction to the icy pavements but only my aching limbs stopped me from falling asleep in the back.

During a long soak in the bath I resolved to keep up with the training and supplement it with the Tae Kwon Do-like balance moves Cole had shown me.

The problem was my feet. Somehow I just wasn't using them as they'd been intended because I found balancing on one leg nearly impossible and relying on them rather than my arms when climbing, counter-intuitive.

I went looking on the Internet for confirmation that I wasn't the only one and came across Andy Coltart's name.

He helps train the British Paraclimbing Squad and in the course of a friendly and highly informative phone-call told me that his visually impaired climbers climb down every wall they ascend as part of their training. This advice was pure gold.

7

Al Alvarez

'Live it up, fill your cup, drown your sorrow
And sow your wild oats while ye may
For the toothless old tykes of tomorrow
Were the Tigers of yesterday.'
                    – from *The Last of the Grand Old Masters*
                                        by Tom Patey

I can't remember exactly when I first read *Feeding the Rat*, but remember the effect it had on me. Here in Al Alvarez was an author and climber who 'got it' – who recognised that some of us only feel truly alive when clinging to a flake of rock at what others regard as a suicidal distance from the ground.

The book's protagonist, Alvarez's sometime climbing partner and friend Mo Anthoine, climbed with all the mountaineers I had come to revere. Content to allow characters like Bonington, Boardman, Whillans and Estcourt to occupy the limelight he was the unsung hero of dozens of epics – an Everyman I could relate to.

Like the fictional heroes of the classic adventure and crime stories I also loved, Anthoine was no death-or-glory merchant; rather he climbed because something gnawing inside drove him to the limits of human endurance; a rat he had to feed.

I have a hazy memory of discussing the book at University with Matt Estcourt, son of the legendary Nick, one stoned-out night in his room, listening to *Dark Side of The Moon*, watched over by a photograph of his long-dead father.

I'd dug my battered first edition out again after that initial conversation with Trevor about the Old Man. He had advised me to go away and reread Alvarez's enthralling account of his own conquest of the stack and then added with casual wistfulness.

'Nice bloke Al Alvarez.'

'What, you know him?' I asked, flabbergasted.

'Yeah, I used to see him around quite a bit, back when I was swimming up at Highgate Ponds, he was a regular – every day. He was a decent climber too, till he shattered his ankle in a fall. Yeah, nice bloke; always had time to stop for a chat.'

With the prospect of climbing the Old Man myself looming large on the horizon I reread his account yet again and determined to find out, from the horse's mouth, exactly what I was letting myself in for.

Knowing that my friend and neighbour Piers Plowright is also an avid outdoor swimmer and frequenter of the Ponds, I'd sought confirmation and was told yes, not only was Al a committed Pond Dipper but also that he lives in the next street!

Piers has the gift of performing effortless introductions between his friends – his confidence that they will find common interest issues an instant bond that he discreetly tops up as conversation develops. He had promised he'd give Al and Ann a call to arrange a time when we could get together for a cup of tea.

However, even Piers cannot orchestrate the iniquities of

health, house-moves and British winter and our attempts had been thwarted so that it was mid-February before we met, and then only briefly at the launch of Al's new book, *Pondlife – A Swimmer's Journal*.

In the meantime, small world that North West London is, Matthew too had become a Pond Dipper and joined the ranks of the East German Ladies Swimming Team (EGLST) whose website justifies their existence better than I ever could:

Inspired by lifelong Highgate Pond Swimmer Al Alvarez (celebrated poet, author, mountain-climber, poker player, and gentleman), a couple of middle-aged Northwest London professionals started swimming in the Highgate Men's Pond in September 2011. As the days started getting colder, friends, acquaintances, and friends-of-friends started joining the weekend swims in theincreasingly-glacial waters.Because the weekly training is carried out in the Highgate Men's Pond, the all-male team decided to honour the most masculine swimming team it could think of: the 1976 East German Ladies Swimming Team, the vanquisher of all opponents at the Summer Olympic Games in Montreal.

These all-weather warriors were out in force amid the crowd thronging the launch at Daunt Books. Piers and Matthew were both there and I was able to perform an introduction of my own and enjoy their animated conversation, before I was whisked off to meet first Ann and then Al himself.

Unfortunately in the excitement no one had told me that Al was in a wheelchair and when we were introduced, the handshake I offered to his face was greeted with a testiness that I recognised from my own reaction to people who fail to notice my white stick. My sense of *faux pas* was compounded when a couple of members of the EGLST, hearing that I too had written a book, promptly bought copies and asked me to sign them.

Despite all this Ann Alvarez, Piers and I agreed that another attempt to meet should be pencilled in for the following week.

Piers was running late and had rung to tell me to go ahead. Frozen slush clung obstinately to the pavement as I slithered the 150 metres from my house to the Alvarez's and wished I had better walking boots than my gripless urban lookalikes.

Over the years I've become accustomed to injury. Regular jarring cranial contact with street furniture, missed kerbstones, potholes and carelessly abandoned objects on the pavement all make for bruising and some-times bloody collisions that I have learned to shrug off and treat with a ready supply of painkillers and arnica. So why was I so worried about an accident now?

Maybe I was feeling sensitive because of the constant ache in my arms and across my shoulders from all the strengthening work. But it was more than that. A new caution had crept into me. I shuffled on.

Ann ushered me through to the sitting room-cum-study at the rear of the house, explaining Al was pretty much confined to the ground floor nowadays. She reintroduced us, gently reminding Al of why I'd come.

Neither his voice nor handshake betrayed a hint of infirmity.

'You must be fucking mad!' he rasped. 'The Old Man's difficult enough when you *can* see! What the hell makes you want to do it?'

'Feeding the rat.' I slid the well-thumbed copy over the table to him. 'Your fault, I'm afraid. You made it sound so . . . compelling.'

He grunted.

'Well most of it looks pretty straightforward,' I said defensively. 'I've watched a couple of ascents on TV and I've tried to get access to a copy of *The Big Climb* through the BFI and by writing to Chris Bonington.'

'If he's got one expect a bill with it' was his reaction to that.

'That big overhang sounds pretty full-on and I'd like to get any information I can before coming face to face with it. Any hints?'

He grunted mirthlessly. '*The Coffin*; it's well-named.'

'It's that bad is it?'

'It's no Sunday picnic. There's nothing too technical about it but there are no good holds. It's a bastard, and that's if you can see what you're doing. Good luck to you!'

It was meant kindly but his gruff delivery and frank amazement at what I was proposing to do was not encouraging.

'Yeah, well you were nearly 60 when you did it. I've got a few years advantage on you. Maybe that evens the odds,' I blurted, before feeling myself redden. The man hadn't been well enough to swim for months now and had made no secret of his frustration at the book launch. Here I was asking him to recall another outdoor passion denied him by his failing body, then getting tetchy when he, quite naturally, pointed out the difficulties my physical limitations may present

He gave a quick, grim laugh. 'I hope you're bloody fit. You'll need to be.'

'Doing a bit more than Egyptian PT anyway' I quipped, making reference to Mo Anthoine's assessment of Al's two weeks lazing in Tuscany before their ascent.

This produced a hearty guffaw that blew much of the tension from the room. 'To be honest with you it's all so long ago I don't remember much about it, other than relief at getting to the top.'

In the few seconds wistful silence that followed I heard his fingers play across the cover of *Feeding the Rat* lying between us.

You don't need to see to know a room is lined with books. Hundreds of thousands of densely packed pages of poetry and prose speak for themselves both in aroma and the sense of insulation they give. Al sat at the centre of this repository of his intellect, experience and achievement, secure in the knowledge that it was all there. If he chose to leave it on the shelf for others to find, because fetching it down made him feel careworn, that was his privilege – a writer's work doesn't lose its power just because the binding's come loose.

Maybe too he was trying to avoid giving me a bum steer like the one he'd felt he received from Bonington's failure to mention a second chimney on the crux pitch in his written account of *The Big Climb*. I decided not to push him further but exit gracefully.

'Well, your vivid description of hanging upside down on the abseil will ensure I check my harness is tight before I descend!'

Again that grim laugh, 'Yes, that was fucking scary . . .' he seemed on the point of elaborating when Piers entered the room, rather breathless and full of apology.

The two men had a lot to catch up on and quickly fell into step on familiar ground; book reviews, local news, poetry; nothing that excluded me, far from it, but it left me feeling as if I'd got to base camp only to be kept there by a discussion about the weather.

'Are Kate and the girls going to come and watch you climb?' It was one of several efforts Piers had made to steer conversation back to the Old Man of Hoy.

I laughed, 'No, I think they'll just be happy to receive confirmation that I'm down safely.'

'Ann's happier now I'm grounded' Al growled and the conversation turned to wives and children and thence to the passage of time and the relative merits of beauty and charm. At the mention of the word both men sighed and in unison quoted Yeats on *Memory*: -

> 'One had a lovely face
> And two or three had charm,
> But charm and face are in vain
> Because the mountain grass
> Cannot but keep the form
> Where the mountain hare hath lain.'

Somehow my copy of *Feeding the Rat* got muddled with one of *Pondlife* that Piers had brought. Amid apologies that this was one of the increasingly numerous days where he couldn't feel his fingers Al's painful, shaky dedication 'To Red, good luck on the climb, Al' ended up on the wrong flyleaf. Piers and I kept this to ourselves as Al slumped back in his chair, oblivious but clearly pissed off with his body's failure to obey the simplest of demands.

With the clock striking six, Ann appeared and offered us all a gin and tonic. Tempted though I was (my abstinence had not progressed into February) I made my excuses and left.

The preceding hour and a quarter had left me with a sharp sense of the short period of time we have to achieve our physical dreams. If on the way home I slipped and fell and broke something I'd lose a year. Twelve months hence what little sight I had would be even less and that which appeared madness to Al now would only become more difficult to achieve.

My future, like Al's present, promised decreasing mobility and while I still could I wanted to go out and grab some stories to furnish my own library in preparation for the dark housebound days that lay ahead.

8

The Cole Styron Workout – Part 2

'It's going to pump your arms like bloated sausages'
— climber, Anthony Burgess

Hi fellas,

Climbing:
Climb! As much as you can. Do endurance sessions where you try to maximise the amount of vertical metres you are climbing regardless of the grade. Do traversing sessions where you see if you can keep your feet off the ground for an hour. Reinhold Messner used to train by going around his stone barn in the Sudtirol until his grip failed. That's the sort of thing we're after.

We're still going to be alternating between the climbing and antagonist muscle groups, however we'll simplify the antagonist stuff a bit. Essentially, for antagonist days, just do your max numbers of crunches and at least 200 press-ups. Try to get the press-ups in as few sets as possible, i.e. it's better to do 4 x 50 than 10 x 20. In addition to that, I'd like you to start adding in lower back extensions. Essentially these involve standing up straight, feet shoulder width apart or slightly wider, hands on head, elbows out to the sides. Bend forward at the waist keeping your back as straight as possible until you are bent 90 degrees and your torso is parallel to the floor. Start with 3x10 sets, but if you find these easy, gradually start adding weight to your hands in the form of single freeweight or a medicine ball or the poor man's version: the gallon jug of water.

Climbing muscle group exercises:

People will tell you that pull-ups don't make the climber and to a degree they're right. However, people live and die by silly mantras all the time, so we're going to ignore them. Overhanging terrain requires good upper body strength; that's all there is to it.

Pull-ups: after warming up, do five sets of your max with 7 minutes rest between. Keep a record of your progress here. If after any three-week period you've shown no improvement, congratulations! That's actually the plateau we're looking for.

After your pull-ups, do a series of lock offs to failure. The first set will be 3x30 degrees. On the second and third pull-up days per week do 3x90 and 3x120 degrees respectively.

In addition to pull-up exercises, when climbing at Swiss Cottage it's probably time to start looking at fingerboard sessions if your tendons allow. I'll need to show you how to do that in person as it's tough to explain. When are you next in at Swiss?

Thanks,
Cole Styron

9

Crack Team

'There are two things that are more difficult
than making an after dinner speech; climbing a
wall that is leaning toward you and kissing a
girl who is leaning away from you'
                                    – Winston Churchill

Andres had been enthusing about the indoor wall at
Brunel for weeks.

'Guys, you've so got to come with me and give it a
go; it's just so cool. It's like someone's cut a big slab of
limestone from the Peak District or somewhere and trans-
ported it down the campus and built a sport hall around
it. There are cracks and ledges and a chimney and an
overhang and this bouldering room that's really cool also.
And it's sooo warm there because it's all indoors. And
there's the student bar also where the beer's really cheap
for afterwards.'

Standing in the semi-shelter of the glass canopy at
Swiss, the rain dribbling down the fibreglass walls and
our breath condensing in front of us, this didn't sound
like a bad idea. Brunel was only 50 minutes away up the
Met Line, and Cole had been insistent that Matthew and I
needed practice on the horizontal and vertical cracks that
are such a feature of sandstone and many other rock types.
In the absence of outdoor routes, courtesy of one of the

wettest winters on record, an indoor facsimile, especially one with beer, seemed a good alternative.

I could tell Matthew was as excited as I when we met at Finchley Road tube station for the first of our three visits. The photos Andres had taken made it look like quite a crag (actually the small figures on the wall proved to be a party of kids!).

We chatted happily about the search for someone to sort the logistics and guide us up the Old Man. Here again Matthew's expertise in research was proving invaluable, the visual strain of trawling for names would have put me right off. Matthew also suggested that I seek sponsorship and/or raise money for charity; neither of which I was keen to embark on until I was sure I stood at least a chance of getting up the stack.

If Cole's training programme had been my first test, then this training wall was the next. And yet I felt pretty confident. I was getting heartily sick of being told that my hand or foot was on the wrong colour hold – they all looked grey to me. On an indoor wall that nullifies the climbing grade of the problem. On an outdoor crag and this realistic copy every hold *was* grey. Just as there are no rules in a knife fight, no holds are barred on a rock face. Tucked away in the back of my mind I kept the reassuring knowledge, gleaned from *Feeding The Rat*, that Al Alvarez had only succeeded in exiting *The Coffin* by lassoing an old wooden wedge left behind after the first ascent.

We met Andres at Uxbridge and caught the bus to the campus. He too was in high spirits and laden with gear, including ropes and at least three pairs of climbing shoes. Matthew's rucksack too groaned weightily and I began to wonder what I'd forgotten to pack. I took firm hold of it and followed my two companions through a labyrinth of walkways that put me in mind of the set of *A Clockwork*

Orange. We arrived at a modern sports hall that was bathed in that queasy half-light common to all high-roofed gymnasia on grey days. Looming from the shadows and occupying the entire far end wall, the 300-square-metre artificial rock-face looked as gloomy as *the Roaches* on a damp Derbyshire morning.

Matthew and I took the obligatory rope safety test to a backbeat of enthusiastic netball practice being conducted on the other side of the partition that separated the wall from the main hall. We both passed technically but I was failed on administrative grounds. I might, in the future, use my competency certificate to book in with other companions and if I belayed them without a competent (sighted) person I risked causing an accident.

Matthew began a patient, if testy, explanation of the number of hours and level to which we had climbed together, while I, incensed at the implicit assumption that my physical disability so impaired my mental capacity that I would seek to endanger the lives of my friends, did my best to keep my mouth shut.

Eventually the clearly embarrassed and flustered instructor held his hands up in defence and said, 'I really don't know what to do here. I can see you know what you're doing, so I can let you climb, as long as one of your two friends is with you at all times. And I suppose you can belay so long as you are accompanied on the ground by one of them.'

'So you're saying he can come in so long as we come with him?' Matthew demanded.

'Yes.'

'Good. We're here; let's climb!'

Andres, who had been watching from the sidelines chorused, 'Yeah dudes, let's climb!' Then asked quietly 'What the fuck was all that about?'

'Just the Health & Safety nanny state protecting the disabled from themselves,' I muttered.

We roped up with irritation and a profound sense of being scrutinised and prepared to tackle the first problem, a ten-metre vertical flake with a few horizontal edges and a handful of pockets, probably only a 4+.

Andres had warned us of the dissimilarity between this and our usual indoor wall but Matthew, who was to go first, was uncharacteristically quiet for a full minute before he started to climb. And, though he'd been out on rock far more recently than me, he puffed and panted his way up.

Rather than give his normal post-match appraisal after I'd belayed him back down (with Andres standing silently at my side) Matthew suggested, 'I know, Andres, let's see how Red does on this without you giving him any instructions.'

It seemed sensible, though in the gloom I needed to be guided across the crash mat to the face of the wall. I gave it a good grope. Much of its surface had been worn smooth by successive generations of students but it still had some texture and the odd wickedly sharp protrusion as if chunks of flint had been cemented into it. The route I was to tackle however was predominantly concave holds that you had to jam your fingers into. Little stood proud of the wall; the opposite of Swiss.

Feeling pumped-up before a climb inevitably leads you to get pumped during it – with the result that you climb like Rambo and knacker your arms. Maybe it was the debacle over the safety test, the fact I was keen to impress or possibly the double shot of coffee Matthew and I had enjoyed before setting out, but within two moves I'd yanked myself up on my, always weaker, right arm and twinged the pectoral muscle. Cursing silently in deference to the children in the hall I hauled my inelegant way to the top and was belayed down as a sweaty mess. It was going to be an educational day.

Andres and Matthew said nothing, which was suspicious in itself, and we moved to the next problem; another ten-metre vertical, with a three-inch crack running down much of its face and a similar horizontal crack at about eight metres. There was a mix of incut and protruding holds, the latter small and widely spaced.

This kind of vertical crack is known as an off-width, being too wide for effective hand or foot jamming, and best climbed by laybacking, *ie*, pulling back on the edge of the crack with both hands and using friction, or any tiny holds you can find, for your feet. This hand-over-hand technique is an art and hard on the arms at the best of times, the more so if they're already pumped.

Matthew and Andres made short work of it. Again I went at it like a bull, making it only to the horizontal crack before flogging myself for five more minutes in a frenzy of flailing and falling, known in climbing parlance as dogging.

I was belayed down, gasping and dejected. This was exactly the kind of thing I would be encountering on the Old Man and it had beaten me.

'You're trying to do it all on your arms. It's not going to work.' Matthew's blunt Yorkshire assessment was spot-on but sounded so like Geoff Boycott that it shot right up my nose and smarted.

'Well, I can't get comfortable on the bloody footholds to reach anything above,' I shot back.

'You need to caress the rock, like it is a woman,' Andres chipped in, which seemed at the time to be the most useless piece of advice he'd ever given.

'You're grabbing anywhere for handholds. You need

to keep your hands on the rock and feel around, like you're feeling a woman all over; like this.' I could only guess at the gyrations his palms were performing and puffed out my cheeks in mingled annoyance and amusement. Teenage tittering came from the netball game behind us.

'Yeah, that's all great but not if my feet aren't a solid platform. There's no good footholds.' I knew I sounded like a petulant workman blaming the tools, but I was pissed off and feeling defensive.

'Let's give it a go blindfolded,' Matthew suggested.

It was a good idea, not least because it allowed me to cool off. By now my eyes had adjusted a little to the light and fortunately both he and Andres were wearing white T-shirts so I had a misty view of their backs moving slowly but inexorably up the dark grey wall in front of me as I paid out the top rope. It took each of them much longer than the first time and, though they both made it to the top, I comforted myself that they had had the advantage of that preview.

Matthew, I noticed, moved deliberately, mostly using his legs to push him up. Andres, like me, used his upper body strength to force his way up but often had his body turned side-on into the wall to stop him barn-dooring (swinging around away from the rock on the arm and leg of one side when the other side loses contact).

Matthew called a timeout and I discovered what was in his over-stuffed bag.

'Eat this.' He thrust a Twix into my hand. I made to protest; I don't have a particularly sweet tooth and I was still trying to lose that extra half stone which wasn't proving so easy with the re-introduction of alcohol to my diet.

'Don't argue. If you're going to do this you're going to

have to learn to eat quick sugars. You don't need to like them but you do need to keep your energy levels up.' I stuffed it down, grateful for the instant, happy rush it gave me.

That was the sweetener. 'Right,' he continued, as soon as my mouth was crammed 'that wasn't so easy. I had to make a lot more, smaller moves. You're trying to go up too fast; it means you're often moving two limbs at a time, that's why you don't feel in balance. You need to slow it down, one limb at a time; remember your three points of contact or you'll wear your arms out and then you'll never get up the Old Man.'

We were sitting on the edge of the crash mat; the netballers had been replaced by the delicate *thwock* of badminton.

'Yeah mate, you gotta think more about placing your feet. If you only rely on your arms you're gonna keep on getting pumped and you'll never get to the top.' I scowled in a 'pot kettle black' way. 'Hey mate, I use my feet too but if you want to build your arms like me you'll need to build your stamina. Every day I do sets of seven pull-ups on the fingerboard, each for seven seconds up then seven seconds down.'

I'd been trying. I was up to three reps of six every other day, holding for about two seconds. Unless I lost another stone and did nothing else but exercise that wasn't going to happen. Matthew thrust some more Twix my way. I might be Andres' height but I was far more Matthew's light build. I wolfed down the chocolate; maybe I should aim to climb more like Matthew.

'I want to look at your shoes mate.' Andres said, picking up my foot. He tutted. 'These are too big. Your toes need to be bent down at the front so you can push into the small holds. What size feet do you have?'

'8½' I said glumly, wondering whether any aspect of my climbing was going to be right today.

'And your shoes?'

'I dunno, 8 I think.'

'Christ. My feet are 9½ and I'm wearing 7½s, no wonder you can't find any edges!' Matthew chimed in. He may as well have said 'Christ, I thought you knew what you were doing, am I trying to get a complete ignoramus up a mountain!'

'Your feet are my size, so why don't you try wearing these?' Andres produced a pair of climbing slippers that would have been a snug fit on my twelve-year-old daughter and I forced my feet into them.

'Comfortable?'

I scowled at Andres. 'As a Chinese princess.' My middle toe on each foot was bent up into a V and all my toenails were being driven back into their cuticles; it was excruciating.

'You'll get used to it. Go and have another try at the crack,' he urged.

I hobbled to the rock face and began to climb.

'Remember, stroke the surface like it's a woman's body.' Andres encouraged from behind, provoking a snort from a young female instructor who had just arrived and come over to watch.

Despite the discomfort my feet felt more at home on the wall. Crunched up my toes gave me more accurate downward pressure and an unbending platform to rest on and push off from. I found I could gain purchase on the thinnest of ledges and create pressure and friction far more easily than before.

I'd stopped fighting the climb and begun to enjoy it, reaching the crux calmly and with some energy still in the tank. This was where I'd got stuck before and my instinct was to force it; to pull up on the horizontal crack then grope blindly above it for a 'thank God' hold to save me.

My right arm, still aching and weak from its earlier abuse, twinged the moment I tried. I ground to a halt, muttering darkly.

Matthew's voice cut sharply across Andres who was urging me on. 'I couldn't do that on my arms so I jammed my leg into the vertical crack and pushed up against that.'

'Ah, like bridging,' I thought, 'now that's something I am good at.' Ten seconds later I was sitting at the top, triumphantly gasping 'Yes, yes, flipping yes!' Beneath the applause from my two companions below I heard Andres confide '6a or maybe 6b, not easy' and my frustration was instantly dispelled.

I hesitate to say it was as if a veil had been lifted from my eyes but thereafter I climbed with a new confidence born of insight. The pain in my arm was a constant reminder to think before relying on it and that of my strangling feet to use them to their full advantage. As the three of us conquered first a problem based round a thin meandering crack that demanded confident, precision footwork, then a steep bulging route that required a succession of rockovers and nimble foot-matches, I felt increasingly in balance, working from a more secure platform with time to explore my surroundings more calmly and methodically, so that I found holds I would otherwise have surely missed. From a dispiriting start it seemed to be turning into one of those days where everything clicks.

After refuelling on Jaffa Cakes (again courtesy of Matthew who I duly appointed Hoy Expedition Quartermaster) we moved the rope along again and prepared to tackle the final section of wall, which lay in the darkest corner.

'I have brought my head torch for you to try' Andres announced as I was tying in.

'It's the newer version of the one you have.' This was his polite way of saying that it was better quality than the one I'd borrowed from my ten-year old daughter.

It was duly fixed to my helmet and I began to inch my way up a steep wall that held a very sparse population of holds, the majority of which were pinches and finger pockets. The torch, though bright, made little difference to what I could see. It reflected straight back off the polished surface below the crux, which required an evil fist-jam and smear up a featureless face and held me up for a couple of minutes. I returned to the mat panting but triumphant.

'I'm loving the light' called the female instructor who was still watching us and had clearly not clocked that I was blind.

I resisted the temptation to give a sarcastic answer along the lines of 'I'm checking for cracks in your wall' and heard her colleague (the one who had performed my safety test) bring her up to speed. A ripple of incredulity ran through the group of kids she was supervising.

While Andres roped up for an attempt on the chimney, I retrieved my water bottle and white stick and tapped my way from one side of the sports hall to the other. When I got back to where Matthew was belaying he asked me whether everything was okay.

'Yeah, fine thanks. Really good.'

He was puzzled. 'Why'd you wander off then?'

'Oh, just giving a practical demonstration for the sceptical' I said, wafting the stick. 'After all, seeing is believing. Now they've seen I'm really blind and that it doesn't stop me climbing, one or two of that lot may go away and think about it and who knows next time they see someone with a white stick they might not be so quick to jump to conclusions.'

A couple of minutes later the instructor who'd done my safety test came over to talk.

'Nice system you've got going there' he said. 'Great communication. When you first came in I really didn't know what to expect . . .' He trailed off, awkwardly.

'Thanks,' I smiled. 'Well I don't guess it's an everyday occurrence.' I explained how we'd got together at Swiss and had a plan 'to climb something quite challenging,' all the time listening with some consternation to the grunts and groans coming from the chimney.

The instructor quizzed me about how much outdoor climbing we, and I guess I in particular, had done, throwing in technical terms that were meant to gauge my level of competence. By now Andres had squeezed his shoulders through the bottleneck top of the chimney and was flat on his back on the crash mat recovering from his exertions.

Matthew sidled off to chat to the female instructor, who likewise seemed finished for the day. I winced when I heard him mention the Old Man by name, and listened for the peal of incredulous laughter. Instead the instructor I'd been talking to whistled then blurted: 'Look I'm sorry again about earlier. I'm bound by the rules you know. One insurance company refused to pay out for an accident at a wall in Reading recently because the climber hadn't filled in the date on the form. There's no question about your climbing, if it was up to me you could do all your training here.'

I assured him there were no hard feelings and he shook my hand and wished me good luck.

Matthew was tying in for his attempt now and I moved over to watch beside a sweaty and aching Andres. The female instructor, clearly still a bit embarrassed, hovered in the background finishing off paperwork. A bevy of teenagers had arrived for archery practice – a couple, according to Matthew sporting Anthrax T-shirts and wielding crossbows. I was glad to discover that they were aiming away from us, after four hours climbing my back hurt enough already.

This noisy, hormone-pumping crowd was, however, silenced by Matthew's expression of frustration and woe as he peeled away from the wall. Having warned me to keep the fruitier end of my vocabulary locked away in the presence of children, his expletive-laden howl echoed percussively around the building.

'Not easy' was his breathless précis on completing the route. 'Here, have some of this, you'll need it' and he thrust another stick of Twix at me.

By now I was expecting failure before I'd cleared my own height. The chimney was a vital aspect of the Old Man; the second pitch is dominated by two of the buggers.

The one in front of me at Brunel was tall and narrow, approached from the left by a short traverse that led into a tight upward-angled crack before rising vertically in a metre-wide flue with occasional jagged protrusions and culminating in a rounded bulge for the climber to squeeze past at the neck, before he can flop onto the ledge at the summit.

No matter how well a climb is outlined to you, it will never describe your own experience of it. Each of us has our own bugbears and specialities.

I began to inch across the narrow ledge towards the dingy mouth of the chimney, glad that the rubber edge of my borrowed shoes was not as worn as the artificial rock face. Wriggling up the tight crack to the base of the vertical, which was slick with use and the sweat of my two companions' laboured efforts, I relaxed. This, I remembered, was what I loved about climbing at Harrison's Rocks when I was a teenager; squeezing along dark, mucky crevices: thrutching up chimneys on chicken-wing arms, knee jams and leg bars; inelegant but perfect for a person of my build; something I could do better than the taller, less-compact Matthew and the chunkier, less flexible Andres.

'Who needs to see when the problem is this tactile?' I thought as I slid round the bulge and mantled, jubilant and barely out of breath, onto the ledge at the top.

'Wasn't the crux on The Old Man just a glorified chimney?' I thought happily, as Andres scuttled off to set the rope for one last problem. Maybe I did stand a chance after all. Until today the project had seemed as artificial as the routes at Swiss. With my progress today and especially my dominance of that last problem the concept had set itself in stone.

We should have called it a day there and then; bagged our achievements and gone and messed about in the bouldering room as Andres had originally suggested but he, and Matthew, were itching to attempt the overhang. With a five-foot wide roof to cross before you could pull yourself up onto the ledge and safety, it was a monster to rival *The Sloth* in the Peak District but without that route's massive jug-handle holds.

Andres nailed it at his third attempt, Matthew turned the air blue during his three goes but only got as far as hanging upside down and groping for the ledge. I didn't even get that far.

We were all tired. I hadn't really understood their description of the route and hadn't had the energy to ask again. Maybe too I was a bit cocky. I got up under the overhang easily enough then just hung there uselessly, my strength bleeding away.

'You need to straighten your arms, you're hanging there on bent arms and legs like a child. Sort it out, Red' shouted Matthew. He was probably just frustrated at his own failure but it really pissed me off.

'Stick your whole arm in the crack and rest on it' shouted Andres. 'Then get your legs high up under the overhang and push out on them so you can reach the edge.'

'There's a hold in the crack over your left shoulder. No, not that side, your left!'

'Straighten your arms, then push out on your legs! No higher!'

'Yes.'

'No! Behind you, over your right shoulder. No, your left; yes, your left shoulder.'

'Not *that* left, Red, the other left!'

'Legs higher and straighten them.'

'Left hand, Red, left!'

Too many voices, too many instructions. I lunged for a non-existent hold and with a howl of exasperation, described a deep pendulum that, satisfyingly, all but knocked Matthew off his feet.

I went up a second time with much the same results except this time I forgot to let go with my right arm and took the full force of my swinging fall in my biceps. The third time I was too weak to reach the crack and gave in with a whimper that left Matthew in hysterics.

Failure had taken much of the sheen off the day for me. It was a painful reminder that the crux of Hoy might only be a glorified chimney but that extra bit of decoration was a bastard big overhang that I'd need to do a lot of work to overcome.

When Matthew had first seen Cole's fitness programme he'd sniffed and declared: 'That's because you are going to need to be at 110% the day we climb. You have no margin for error, we do.'

What had seemed smug then, now made sense. He'd

out-performed me having done little of the strengthening work I had over the past weeks and carrying a niggling shoulder injury. No matter how hard I trained I could never be over-prepared.

Up in the refectory everyone's spirits rallied with some food and drink. Still, I was hardly in celebratory mood and so opted for a pint of Coke to wash down a surprisingly good burger as we discussed what we'd learned over our four and a half hours of climbing and what our next steps should be.

'Well, at least we now know who is in charge of supplies, Matthew.' I began light-heartedly. 'Thanks for thinking to bring all those snacks, it never occurred to me.'

'It's the good Jewish mother in me' he grimaced. 'You're going to have to get used to eating all sorts of crap you know. Like Cole said, endurance bars are no joke. You need to experiment with them and find which ones don't make you retch. And you can't keep gulping down water all the time. It's not going to be so easy to go for a piss on the Old Man, you've got to learn to take small sips.' As with water so with wine I thought ruefully.

'And you're going to have to get comfortable hanging off your arms when they're wedged in a crack and to having your head forced over to one side under an overhang.'

'Yes, mum.'

The lecture continued. 'You're not always going to have a choice where you take your rests. On the subject of which have you followed Cole's advice and tried hanging in a harness for fifteen minutes at a time yet?' His tone suggested he knew the answer already.

It was fair comment. He'd seen limitations in my performance and was keen to flag them while it was all still fresh in the mind. It was done with the best of intentions but my self-confidence needs to be fed with equal doses of honey and lemon, especially when I'm tired, so my spirits plummeted again; the more so because I knew he was right.

'Oh, fuck it Matthew. The whole thing may collapse before we get there,' I snapped, keen to change the subject. 'Or when we're halfway up.'

'What!?' Andres struggled to keep up with irony at the best of times. Unlike Matthew, in whom black humour was ingrained, I tended to go easy on him. So when I came out with comments like this he knew it was odds on that I wasn't joking and his horror now was palpable.

Matthew and I took some delight in explaining the geology and temporary nature of sea stacks; information I felt sure Andres would check on his iPhone as soon as he was alone. Eventually, after another pint, he reconciled himself to this previously uncalculated danger and threw it back at me. 'Well, we better climb it sooner than later then, hey Red?'

It was another job on my to-do list. Matthew had sifted the British Mountaineering Council (BMC) directory and rung around to establish which of their qualified Mountain Guides had experience of leading an expedition to Hoy. The next step, interviewing them over the phone, fell to me and I'd been putting it off, worried that my climbing might not be up to standard.

As if reading my mind, Andres said, 'There's no doubt you could do it mate. You were climbing 6a and b standard today and the wall here isn't so different to rock as Swiss. You just need to work on your technique a little, but I can help you do that. I can set some special routes for you back at Swiss that make you concentrate on your footwork and rock-overs. You'll be fine.'

Somewhat cheered I got my diary out and we came up with a list of possible dates for the climb as well as pencilling in another day at Brunel. On the way back to the

Underground Matthew clapped Andres on the back and declared, 'You should be commended for your charity work.'

I bristled at the word.

'Do you realise that the combined ages of me and Red is 91. You are taking two old men up the Old Man!'

I laughed, mostly at myself for jumping to conclusions about what he'd meant, though my aching body found more truth in his jest than was comfortable.

We returned to Brunel twice before the weather improved enough to head to the outdoor crags. On the first occasion it was just me and Matthew, as Andres was visiting his family in Colombia. The same instructors were there as before and, in a gap between children's parties, Ben, as I found he was called, gave us a master-class in crack climbing; teaching us how and when to use thumbs-up hand jamming methods or thumbs-down elevator door technique, if lay-backing is not possible. Those 20 minutes tuition were amongst the best I have ever received and proved invaluable for my trip to the Scottish Highlands a few weeks later.

Andres was back for our final visit and, fitter, leaner and technically far beyond our abilities of three months before, we set about the routes, knocking them off in a fraction of our previous time and thoroughly enjoying ourselves.

Eventually only the overhang remained.

Matthew went up and over its huge protuberant lip at his first attempt, with a minimum of swearing and something approaching gracefulness, leaving me with mixed feelings of delight and envy.

I got close; so close that I even felt comfortable and relaxed hanging from the roof like a human spider and planning my next move. But in that position no one has more than a limited time to identify and grip the holds and being able to see their whereabouts saves a lot of groping about. I got my hand round the relevant lump of rock eventually on my second attempt up there, but by then my arms were so drained of energy that when I tried to close my grip my fingers splayed as if they were made of perished rubber.

This time though it wasn't anger but disappointment that I felt. The overhang was a boring reminder that no matter how good I got I would only ever climb to the limit of my disability. But in the past few months I'd pushed that limit a long way back and there was time to go yet.

10

Seeking Professional Help

> 'I may say that this is the greatest factor – the
> way in which the expedition is equipped – the
> way in which every difficulty is foreseen, and
> precautions taken for meeting or avoiding
> it. Victory awaits him who has everything in
> order.'
>
> – Roald Amundsen, *The South Pole*

Matthew had approached the task of finding someone
to lead our expedition with customary diligence. His
research indicated that we would be best off with a British
Mountain Guide, a qualification so highly regarded
that holders are in regular demand to lead expeditions
worldwide.

He had narrowed it down to a shortlist based on prox-
imity either to London or the Highlands. The former were
centred around the Peak District which is only about three
hours by car from North London and where we hoped to
get some practice when the weather improved; the latter
would be most likely to have climbed the Old Man before
or have a better idea of the logistics involved.

Of these two desirables Matthew was more concerned
about the logistics and I about getting significant climb
time with the individual. Matthew had studied the map
and we both knew that *The Big Climb* expedition had been

a mammoth operation. Admittedly we were not going to need to employ the British Army to transport a mobile TV studio with us but the last thing we wanted was to get to the foot of the stack only to find that we'd left some vital piece of equipment on the mainland.

What played on my mind though was the uniqueness of the task and the need to get time at the rock face with whomever we gave the job to. I didn't want him (or her) getting cold feet on the crux pitch because they hadn't fully appreciated what they were undertaking. And as much as they needed to feel comfortable with me, I needed to feel comfortable with them. Good communication had after all proved a key factor in raising my performance.

As a former ski instructor Matthew was adamant that this should not be an issue; once he's signed up, a professional gets on with the job no matter what he feels about the individual client; but he agreed that I needed to interview the possible candidates once he had rung round them to gauge their interest.

As it was, our shortlist shortened itself as one name kept coming to the fore whenever the Old Man of Hoy was mentioned.

'Martin Moran is your man . . . . I'd love to take you up there myself, it sounds like a great project, but Martin's the man for the job . . . He must have climbed The Old Man at least ten times,' was pretty much the unanimous response from the half-dozen BMG's Matthew called. The only exception being a former Royal Marine who clearly thought Matthew sounded soft and demanded; 'You're not poofs are you? I don't lead poofs up mountains!'

Softly spoken Tyneside tones answered the phone, which threw me a bit as I had rung a Lochcarron number so was expecting Martin to be a Scot. Had I done my due diligence and checked his informative website I would have known better. He allowed me to blather on about my level of ability, the impact of my disability, my lack of recent outdoor experience, my concerns (mostly centring around the overhang) and the plan to have Matthew, Andres and I all making the ascent together. After about five minutes of listening to my rambling monologue he cleared his throat and ventured;

'Yes, I've spoken to Matthew about the additional challenges but I think we can get you up there. I've been running a Sea Stack Climbing Tour for a number of years and I've had a lot of experience on the Old Man of Hoy. The original East Face route would probably be the best for your attempt. The only really challenging section is on the second pitch but we can lay the optimum route for you and if you're having too many problems on the crux we can always fix on some Jumars and you can jug up. There's no point in allowing a tricky section to spoil a good day's climbing.'

This was music to my ears. Although I was determined that it wouldn't come to that (using clamps to haul myself around and over the Old Man's bulging belly really would feel like cheating) it was good to hear that there was an alternative to having to give up and abseil down if the going got too tough.

I could see why Matthew had come away from his conversation with Martin satisfied that he could be the man for the job. Both saw logistics as the key to success and liked to plan for every eventuality well in advance. Martin's easy preparedness to resort to artificial climbing aids left me in no doubt that the equipment he would provide for the expedition would be comprehensive and I envisaged a climbing rack bristling with every cam, hex and nut available and Matthew and Andres drooling over such an array of kit.

'Of course I'd need to climb with you beforehand so that I can get a sense of what we need to do differently and to get used to the communication system that Matthew says you use. Any chance you can get up to Scotland for a few days?'

I explained that we'd been hoping to stay closer to home and wondered whether he could meet us in the Peak District.

'Oh, I don't need to see all of you. Just you will be enough. And Scotland would be easier for me.'

'That might be tricky,' I explained. 'I look after the kids full-time and my wife's job is very demanding. Do you know anyone in the Peaks who could at least give me an initial assessment to establish whether I'm deluding myself about the Old Man? I don't want to waste anyone's time.'

'Mmm. The Peak District's a good idea. You'll be using many of the same techniques on gritstone as on sandstone. I can put you in touch with some guys at Peak Mountain Training who will be able to assess whether you are climbing near the right grade. If you want to spend time training with one of them and use him as your guide on the climb itself I'd be happy to have any of them as a second on the Old Man with us. Otherwise I can use one of my guys up here.'

'So we'll need two guides will we?' I sensed costs could be rising.

'Yes. I think in this instance, it would be advisable. One to lead the climb and set the protection and a second climbing in parallel with you, in case you get into difficulties.'

I had envisaged Andres doing this but on reflection saw that Martin's suggestion assumed control of both ends of the rope for his team, so minimising risk to his client. Still

I had to minimise costs so thought I'd check with Cole whether there was anyone at Swiss who might be up to the job of seconding. I mentioned this to Martin and his hesitation spoke volumes.

'Do you have any footage of you climbing to give me an idea of the system you run?' he asked, changing the subject. 'Matthew mentioned two-way radios.'

'Afraid not. But if you want a general idea of the effects of RP there's a good description on the RP Fighting Blindness website. They're the charity that deals specifically with Retinitis Pigmentosa and they have loads of information and links.' I stopped short of recommending he read my book, not least because no one in their right mind would take Joe Wynde climbing.

'Well, I might be heading south to visit family over Easter, so it's possible I could meet up with you for a couple of days climbing then. In the meantime you need to spend as much time on rock as possible. Indoor walls are good for keeping fit when you can't get out but they are no substitute. Get in touch with Peak Mountain Training and spend some time up there working on technique, especially on cracks. I'll let you know about getting together in April.'

'Sure, that could work well Martin. My wife and kids are off to Tenerife for ten days over Easter so I'm free then too.'

'Right, good. And I think I should go ahead and book the hostel on Hoy for three nights in June. It's only a small place and it can get booked out quickly during the summer.'

'Does the Old Man get busy?' I had visions of queuing for the summit, as had been reported from Everest that week.

'Occasionally you find another party climbing. But

there are other routes up, so it's not the end of the world. There's another E1, a 5c so a similar grade, on the South Face. But it's best to book the hostel early. I'll reserve the whole place if I can. It only sleeps eight so it doesn't make much difference to the overall cost and it sends the message to anyone else thinking of climbing the same week that there's already a party there. Also it means we'll have room if you decide to bring anyone else with you.'

After a few minutes discussing cost we got to fixing a date for the expedition.

'The weather up there can be a bit unreliable so I'd recommend having a window of three days, then we stand a good chance of getting at least one day we can climb. Also I'd suggest that we go up around midsummer's day, that way there are 18 hours of sunlight, so even if we lose a morning to the weather we can still use the afternoon and evening. The rock dries off quickly in the wind, especially if there's a bit of sun on it.'

We agreed on the 19th, 20th and 21st of June 2013 and I put the phone down with the mixed feelings of a man who has just committed (with worrying ease) to a major life decision such as marriage or a house purchase. Exhilaration and fear played leapfrog in my stomach as I stood alone in my metropolitan kitchen, hail bouncing off the double-glazing, and considered the prospect that lay a mere 16 weeks ahead.

One thing I was sure of though, Martin Moran was absolutely the right man to lead me there.

'That's excellent!' Matthew seemed more delighted with my progress on this front than that on the physical side of the project. Within 24 hours he had extracted the names and numbers of three Peak Mountain Training instructors from Martin and begun urging me to chase them up.

The trouble with the Peak District is that it offers limited possibilities for winter climbing, driving its guides to higher ground to earn an honest crust. Even in the Swiss Alps, mountains and glaciers present an obstacle to mobile and broadband access which made my efforts to track these guys down feel more like a Yeti hunt.

One by one I ran them to ground, only to cross their name off the list. Each was either busy until mid-April or already booked on other work during June. And all the time, to add to our frustration, the rain bucketed down across Britain in the wettest spring for 100 years, washing away any chance of climbing outdoors.

With news of the final guide's regretful apology Martin swung into action.

Dear Red

I am sorry that both Dave and James have effectively pulled out of this venture; but it makes things simpler. My company will organise guides and logistics for both training and the Old Man climb.

I will arrange a guide who is based in North Wales to provide training days (either in Snowdonia or the Peak) and will try to ensure that he can come up to Hoy to guide the climb as well to provide the required continuity. I'll get back to you as soon as I have this organised.

I will also be available in April in Scotland to provide rock climbing up here over a long weekend if you can spare the time to come north.

I think you can easily manage with just two guides on Hoy. To be honest two guides can work much better as a team than three. One of the guides can do the Old Man a second time if your supporting friends want to complete the climb as well.

For the Old Man climb we have booked Rackwick

Hostel from Tues 18th to Fri 21st June. We have exclusive use of the hostel and the price is c£70 per night.

Travel days will be Tues 18th and Sat 22nd. On Tues 18th we will take the evening ferry from Scrabster to Stromness dep 19.00 and on Sat 22nd the mid-morning ferry that departs Stromness 11.00 arr Scrabster 12.30. That means that you need to be in Inverness early afternoon on the 18th and plan a late-afternoon/early-evening return flight to London on the 22nd.

Suggested schedule would be:–
Tues June 18th: meet Inverness 14.00, drive to Scrabster (3hr), take evening ferry to Stromness; dinner, B&B in Stromness

Wed June 19th: take car ferry to Hoy (dep Houton 09.25); drive to Rackwick Hostel; walk to Old Man and recce approach

Thurs and Fri June 20th and 21st: Climb the Old Man
Sat June 22nd: car ferry to mainland (dep Lyness 09.00); ferry to Scrabster 11.00 arr 12.30; drive to Inverness with airport drop-off at 15.30.

Please get in touch if you have any questions. I look forward to receiving your booking and to making the commitment to get the project up and running.
Best regards
MARTIN MORAN

We had lost an entire month waiting both for replies and for the weather to improve. I'd still got no closer to a rock face than climbing at Brunel and was no nearer receiving confirmation that my dream of following in Joe Brown's footsteps was not pure folly. For once my frustration rivalled Matthew's.

I reread the email; weighing up the options and marvelling at the level of fitness Martin and his guides must maintain to propose that one of them should effectively climb each pitch twice in order to lead Matthew and Andres up behind us.

After a cup of tea and a quick chat with my wife, I picked up the phone and had the conversation with Martin that I suspected he thought we should have had in the first place.

'Hi, Martin, it's Red. Look, thanks for the email. To be perfectly honest Snowdonia's no good for me because I'm completely reliant on public transport. I think I'd be best off catching a plane up to Inverness and meeting you there. That way we can have a few days climbing together and you can see firsthand exactly what I can and can't do.'

'Great. I'll have a think and come back to you with an itinerary. When were you thinking of?'

The dates fitted neatly with his schedule and I sensed a relief that mirrored my own. Within a month the uncertainty that hung over the whole endeavour would finally be removed and each of us could get on with making plans for the summer.

11

Highland Fling

'People ask me, 'What is the use of climbing Mount Everest?' and my answer must at once be, 'It is of no use.' There is not the slightest prospect of any gain whatsoever. ... If you cannot understand that there is something in man which responds to the challenge of this mountain and goes out to meet it, that the struggle is the struggle of life itself upward and forever upward, then you won't see why we go. What we get from this adventure is just sheer joy. And joy is, after all, the end of life. We do not live to eat and make money. We eat and make money to be able to live. That is what life means and what life is for.'

– George Mallory

Chief among my reasons for not going to Tenerife with Kate and the kids is the dent in my enjoyment of unfamiliar places caused by the inevitable flurry of accidents that befall me in the first few days of orientating myself. So, for the past couple of years, I'd encouraged the girls to take their annual foreign holiday without me. Laura and Meg get some quality mummy-time and the three of them are freed from being constantly vigilant for a grumpy daddy who feels thoroughly dislocated and guilty for wrecking everyone's holiday.

If I'm going to twist an ankle or get covered in cuts and bruises I'd prefer to do so on my own terms, without a concerned audience and undertaking an activity I enjoy. Kate was happy that I wouldn't be sitting at home (or in the pub) beating myself up over my lack of progress on the novel and reassured that I'd be climbing with someone as professional and well-qualified as Martin. Having seen the ascents he listed on his website she, her parents and my Dad all felt confident that I was in expert hands and was most likely to return in one piece.

Their only real concern was that I would be disappointed if I didn't make the grade. The thought was no stranger to my mind either but I reasoned that it was better to know one way or the other. I was sick of hanging in limbo, my plans to get to the Peaks with Matthew, Andres and the Rusty Peg Climbing Club (who centred around Swiss) constantly thwarted by the crap weather. Booking the air-ticket to Inverness and getting my kit together felt like taking control of a situation that had been allowed to drift for too long.

Besides, Martin had clearly put some thought into creating an itinerary that would be both fun and challenging during which I would be well-supported.

Dear Red

I have arranged a second guide for the Old Man climb. Nick Carter is a qualified MIC instructor living in Inverness, who climbs at a high standard and has done the Old Man several times. Nick has worked for me over several years and is an ideal man for the task.

If you arrive on Tues April 2nd at 11am we can go straight out and do some climbing that afternoon. That means you can get the three days' climbing and return to London on Fri 5th.

Nick is available on Tues 2nd and Thurs 4th, I can do all three days and my son Alex will help me on Wed 3rd. Alex is himself a qualified mountain instructor.

Plan would probably be to climb on the outdoor sports crag at Moy on Tuesday, then we would climb on a sandstone outcrop on Wednesday doing crack climbs, and if the weather is good and all is going well, we will try the classic Cioch Nose of Applecross on Thursday. This is a big multi-pitch route which involves a steep approach and lots of scrambling so would be a perfect dry run for the Old Man.

We have arranged two nights' accommodation for you in Lochcarron at Pathend B&B on Tues 2nd and Wed 3rd. The proprietor Adrian Elliman works for us as cook on our Scottish courses and we will ask if he can make your evening meals.

After climbing on Thursday Nick will drive you back to Inverness and he has booked you into Ardlair Guest House. You can arrange to eat out at nearby restaurants on Thurs evening.

I am much looking forward to the three days with you.
Best regards
MARTIN

I had heard of Applecross before. The pass formed the second highest road in Britain and gave my vertigo-suffering mother-in-law kittens when she had to drive over it. The great Tom Patey who, with Chris Bonington and Rusty Baillie, had made the first ascent of the Old Man of Hoy in 1966, on completing his conquest of the *Cioch Nose*, had written 'what a magnificent climb! It was the Diff to end all Diffs!'

I went surfing, found half a dozen climbing logs on it and Moy Crag and began to read hungrily.

When viewing other people's accounts of climbs they have completed, it is as well to remember that the vast majority of accompanying photos will have been taken from an angle that cannot fail to make the rock look more impressively perpendicular than it actually is, and which often obscures the smaller features that make the ascent possible.

The up-face shots of *The Cioch Nose*, especially the one of a solo climber stepping un-roped round a corner bulge and seemingly into space, made the wall look far more daunting than its 4a grading. Both that and the website I found about Moy Crag gave me that twinge of vertigo I always get when I see others climb but have no idea of their level of competence.

If I felt any anxiety at my own physical preparedness it was subsumed by concerns about my material readiness when, six days before the trip I received the following message from Martin:

Weather is very cold here but bone dry and the snow-line is well up the hill. We must hope it is a bit warmer come next week but we can definitely rock climb in current conditions.

Bring warm kit and full shell garments, including one pair of warm gloves/mittens and one pair of durable gloves for abseiling and belaying.

We will try to give you a rough or steep approach walk on one of the days as a tester for the Old Man approach (eg the Cioch Nose has a 90 minute approach) so bring walking boots and trekking poles.

Bring some snacks for the first day. Adrian will provide some packed lunch for the second and third days. Bring your thermos – Adrian will fill it for you.

'Bloody hell' I thought, 'it must be bitter if a man who has spent half his life in the Alps and Himalayas says 'the weather is very cold'!'

I'd been keeping a wary eye on the forecast around Inverness, happy to note that rain was nowhere to be seen and the temperature was well above freezing. A quick investigation of the map revealed that Applecross lay on the opposite side of The Highlands and, while equally dry, was many degrees chillier.

Matthew had foreseen some of this and bought me a mixed bag of what he called 'bonk bars and spunk' – high energy cereal bars and power gels aimed at delivering a huge carb and sugar boost just when you feel your head drop and are convinced you can't go on. Designed for ultra-marathons and the like, they made me feel a bit of a fraud as I packed them in beside the family pack of Snickers that I had equipped myself with. Still, like the Jumars, it was good to know that they lay in reserve.

He had also lent me a good thick fleece and a pair of old ski-gloves that he said he didn't mind me wrecking. But this didn't sound like it would be enough.

Technical clothing is expensive and I was reluctant to borrow anything I'd be worried about damaging. Swiss is so cold in the winter that I already had thermal tops and longjohns to go under the excellent climbing trousers and Gore-Tex anorak that Kate had given me as birthday and Christmas presents, but the need to source 'shell garments' played on my mind.

I was running on a tight budget and things kept cropping up. My experience at Brunel coupled with a hole in the old pair had forced me into buying new climbing shoes and this with the necessity for a helmet and the cost of the trip to Inverness, meant I really couldn't afford to rush out and buy high-cost items that I may only ever wear once. Fortunately Cole and Oxfam came to my rescue.

I'd hoped to borrow a down jacket from Swiss. The ones used by the instructors were torn and patched already and I reckoned the weather had warmed up enough in London that they could do without one of them for a long-weekend. Cole felt that he couldn't loan High Sports property but was happy to lend me a bright yellow one of his own that fitted as if it had been tailored for me.

'Cole, I can't possibly. This must be a £200 jacket.'

'Hey, fuck it man. Someone's gotta put a hole in it sometime. Just don't smoke anywhere near it, okay?'

Determined not to let anything near it, I went shopping for something to wear over it. In the Oxfam shop at the end of my road I found a brand new shell fleece (still with its tags) for a tenner. Feeling lucky I asked the manager whether she had any ski-trousers and within five minutes was the happy owner of a pair of snowboarding pants that cost me even less! They were mildly garish but left me feeling equal to whatever the Scottish weather might throw at me.

Kate and the girls left on the Friday and I had the weekend to pack and repack and let my excitement build. It reminded me of when I went backpacking across Andalucía to Gibraltar, during the last summer before I learned that I wasn't simply short-sighted. I love travelling light, eking things out so you use less and the tight planning that entails. I even found myself looking forward to the journey.

On any other day getting up before dawn to catch a plane would be my nightmare but I was out of bed before the alarm went off and happy to be on my way. Every section of my journey was smoothed by someone offering help or guidance or simply company, making my adventure through a maze of movement and shadows fun rather than fearful.

A little over three hours after leaving my house I was arm in arm with a stewardess walking towards the baggage carousel at Inverness Airport.

'I can take over from here if you like.' The speaker was tall, muscular and spoke with a strangely familiar accent. 'Hi, you must be Red, I'm Nick.' He had a climber's handshake; one that is firm, never seeks to crush, but retains the ability to support the entire weight of the attached body using only a finger or two.

'I'm parked just outside' he said swinging my rucksack onto his broad shoulders, 'Good trip?'

It turned out Nick grew up in Eastbourne, the other end of Sussex to me, and had also cut his climbing teeth at Harrison's. We were about the same age, both married, he with one daughter me with two, and hit it off immediately. The weather, which had been grizzly in London, was glorious as we drove out through the Dingwall countryside towards a destination described by ScottishClimbs. com as:

Moy Rock is a conglomerate south facing crag, north of Inverness. Currently there are a number of trad routes for those with a death wish and 16 sport routes that have been fully equipped and climbed. In the area that has been developed, the nature of the rock and the lack of any protection lends itself well to an ideal sport climbing venue. There is also potential for bouldering.

I had perused the list of routes, which included a 6a+* tantalisingly called *The Old Man of Moy*. Though none was prefixed by an F, I could only assume they were sports grades. Otherwise there was a worrying scarcity of lower grade climbs on which to warm up and build confidence.

Martin cut a lean, intense figure, waiting by the silver Moran Mountain minibus; compact in the type of climbing gear that is so unflashy that you know it is top quality. I squinted hard as we approached, trying to focus, and received a quick smile that revealed white teeth set in a healthy, weather-beaten face. Like his handshake it was brief and business-like. We exchanged a few words about travel and conditions before he said, 'Well, if you're ready to climb let's go on up.'

I've read enough autobiographies and heard enough interviews to know that conserving energy is second nature to mountaineers; waste is anathema to them. So I took Martin's reserved manner as a sign of his professionalism.

It did though, make me feel excessively self-conscious as I proceeded to strew the contents of my rucksack across the lay-by. I am neat and tidy by nature and had packed so that the items I would need to climb were folded close-at-hand. I had not however reckoned on it being 12 degrees C and bright sunshine.

'Let's have a look at your boots,' he said quietly, as I rammed my newly acquired snowboarding trousers and fleece into the chaos I'd made of my bag.

'No grip' he sniffed, turning them over then placing them on the tailgate. 'And you'll need something with more support for the walk in. What size do you take?'

'8½, 9' I was feeling a complete bloody amateur now, with my urban walking boots, fit only for the well-kempt paths of Hampstead Heath.

I received a pair of high ankle mountain boots, made a mess of lacing them up and had to suffer the ignominy of having them tied for me. Finally we were ready to scramble up the approach. Much of the slope had been cleared of trees and was pitted with stumps and hollows, but it was dry and there was a reasonably well-worn trail. The crag loomed above us, deserted save for its vocal bird population.

'Right let's get you warmed up on something' Martin said. 'What do you reckon, Nick?'

They chose a steep slab with a wide groove running jaggedly from base to summit; beginner's stuff but being conglomerate rock (Nature's equivalent to pebbledash), abrasive and unforgiving should you fall. On the plus side it is great for smearing up (using the friction of the soles of your shoes instead of footholds).

Now I struggled to tie myself in and was glad Martin was busy sorting out the rope and quickdraws. As I struggled to find the loop at the base of my harness I felt a rising frustration at my inadequacy. Matthew's words from the week before came back to me.

'Remember, slow down, concentrate, check and ask Martin to double-check your rope safety; it will put his mind at ease, and yours. I've worked as a ski instructor and there's nothing worse than someone who thinks they know it all, won't accept advice and puts themselves and everyone else in danger. Ask. Even if it makes you feel stupid it will make Martin confident knowing you're safe.'

'Nick, sorry to ask but something's wrong with the loop on my harness, I can't seem to feed the rope through.' I was loath to take the harness off having taken an age to sort out the leg-loops already. Nick began to fiddle with the nylon tie at my crotch.

'The buckle's bent. Have you taken a fall recently?'

A bruise on my shin, the shape and colour of a Victoria plum, could bear testament to that. After Matthew had departed on holiday the previous week I had needed a climbing partner for my Thursday session and hooked up with a guy with macular degeneration who also climbs at Swiss. We enjoyed an hour of the blind leading the blind until, on an ambitious 6a, we had both failed to spot a very necessary hold and I had come crashing down after a dynamic leap.

'That's got it. Not surprised you couldn't fix that. I found it tricky,' Nick reassured.

With Martin perched about ten metres above and Nick belaying, I psyched myself down for a slow, steady ascent. I always dislike the first couple of moves, the potential for falling and twisting an ankle or taking your face off on the rock feels greater when there is less distance for the rope to run out or stretch before you hit the ground. After a slightly scrambled start I soon struck a rhythm and within five minutes was staring at Martin's boots. He gave a satisfied grunt and lowered me back down again.

The next two routes steadily increased the grade, and my confidence. I was feeling comfortable on the rock. The south-facing crag was a natural suntrap and soon we had all shed our layers, enjoying the warmth and light that had been in hibernation since the previous October. London, its pollution and stress levels, seemed a thousand miles away and I was as genuinely happy as on any holiday since my honeymoon.

We stopped for a bite to eat and I pulled out my home-made sandwiches, apple and a bonk bar. Martin looked approvingly at the first two items but refused a chunk of the energy booster.

'Aye, I've tried those on Everest, or something like them. I'll stick to my wife's cake thank you.'

Nick took a bit and pronounced it 'Not as bad as some' before polishing off his chocolate bar.

After this I was given a lesson in Prusiking (an artificial climbing technique and alternative to Jumaring achieved by winding a nylon cord with a locking knot round the rope to form a looped slipknot that can be slid up the rope but tightens fast as soon as downward pressure is applied). Using this for my hand and its mechanical equivalent, a Ropeman with a sling, for my foot, I made sweaty panting progress up a route it had taken a fraction of the time to climb with my bare hands before lunch.

'Looks like you're getting the hang of it' Martin called up. 'That's the method we'll use if you get stuck on the overhang'.

'Bugger that. It'll have to be pretty hairy to force me into doing this again' I shouted back. 'Can I do some proper climbing now please?'

The sun was blazing and we were joined by a couple of local regulars. Martin introduced me but said nothing about my sight until I was halfway up the next route, which turned out to be *The Old Man of Moy*, a vertical, narrow crack with a nasty bulge at the top. It took time, not helped by coming the wrong side of the penultimate quickdraw and having to unclip with my right hand back to front and my left slipping out of a two-finger pocket. I made it to the top and returned only a little shakily to the bottom.

'Good lad,' said Martin.

'Aye, good effort. Good luck on Hoy, man. Wish I could be with you,' said one of the locals.

'Fancy trying something a bit more challenging?'

I paused; in Martin's lexicon I suspected 'a bit more challenging' lay with the superlatives. My arms were still pumped after my tussle with the quickdraw but I was climbing well and took his suggestion as a compliment.

Moy Bueno turned out to be a pumpy slog of an F6b; steep (*ie*, leaning in towards me) from bottom to top. The holds, though by no means scarce, were awkward; small pinches and pockets that, because of the unrelenting steepness of the wall, I had to take rather than have time to seek alternatives. The crack, when I reached it, afforded some relief but was too narrow for a decent foot-jam and kept me moving up and hoping to find wider purchase.

About six feet from the top I ran out of steam. The final bulge was pushing into my face, forcing me backwards and I could find no foothold to take me high enough to reach over it for holds that I suspected would be anything but jug-handles.

'I'm coming down! I think I should save myself for tomorrow.'

But there was no sense of defeat, just of a battle well-fought and to be continued.

'You climbed well today' said Martin, his unexcitable voice betraying a hint of surprised pleasure. 'I think we could give *Cioch Nose* a try tomorrow, how would you feel about that?'

I was elated, though fortunately too knackered to do more than grin and accept the invitation.

12

The Diff to End all Diffs

'It's a wonderful feeling to push even a tiny
piece of the planet down beneath one's feet.'
– Adrian Burgess

'You lucky sod!' The text was from Paul, another dad
from school and keen climber who knew Applecross
well. It preceded the alarm I'd set by a good 20 minutes,
but I'd been awake since dawn, too excited to go back to
sleep.

At seven pitches and 200 metres high the climb I was
taking on today would be by far the longest I had ever
attempted and, if I didn't make a mess of it, should give
me the green light for the Old Man of Hoy in June.

My mobile trilled with another message, this time from
Matthew wishing me a simple 'Good luck.'

After a comprehensive and filling breakfast (I never
have problems clearing my plate and suspected I'd need
every calorie on offer) I did my best to empty my bladder
fully and waited for Martin who was punctual and accompanied by his son Alex.

'The sirens going out to the wild-fires didn't keep you
awake then?' Martin asked, after he'd enquired whether
I'd had a good night's sleep.

'No, dead to the world' I replied. Actually I'd fallen
asleep listening to a Sherlock Holmes on my iPod but had

wondered why the morning air had smelled so heavily of smoke.

'The landowners start them to clear the scrub and then they get out of hand. It happens every year. Fortunately it shouldn't affect us where we're going today.' He was positively chatty, more relaxed than the previous day.

It was a beautiful, crisp morning. Smudges of smoke and cloud hung in an otherwise clear blue sky. I chatted with Alex as Martin navigated the twisting loch-side road and learned that he was in his early twenties and teaching at a school in Edinburgh. The previous year he'd been working at Gordonstoun with another outdoor sports and climbing instructor who had found out he had R.P.

'Poor sod' I said, 'that's his livelihood up the swanee. How did he take it?'

'Hard at first I think, but he's got a strong support network round him and he's good friends with Andy Kirkpatrick and Karen Darke.'

'Well they should keep him inspired,' I said. 'But tell him to get in touch if he ever wants a natter . . . or a moan.'

The miles slipped by and the peaks grew taller and more snow-capped as conversation flowed easily between the three of us. As fellow locals and fellow climbers they knew Andy Fitzpatrick fairly well and we had all recently watched the episode of the BBC's *My Life* in which his daughter had Jumared up El Capitan. Alex had also watched the episode in which my daughter, Laura, had talked about having prosopagnosia (face blindness).

Some days everything seems to click together, so by the time we pulled into the car park I was feeling part of a team, relaxed and confident of a successful day's climbing in perfect conditions; happy to listen and follow Martin and Alex's lead.

Which was just as well. The compacted snow covering

the car park was like an ice-rink. My Timberland boots would have deposited me in the valley 700 feet below had I not again swapped them for Martin's pair, and I came to thank his foresight all the more on the 45 degree scramble down into the gully beyond.

This was the part that I (and it turns out Martin) had been dreading. I find going down stairs difficult enough and regularly stumble when walking off kerbs. Even with the trekking pole Martin had advised me to bring, and a short rope attaching my harness to his, providing a modicum of added security, the going was gruelling.

Maintaining your balance while crossing uneven ground requires sight. Without it you end up disoriented and relying on your arms as much as your legs. Going uphill isn't so bad, but descent is perilous; if you stumble it's headfirst down into the next obstacle, if you slip you fall backwards into the last one. I did most of it crablike, clambering down on my backside using my arms for support, grateful to Matthew for his ski-gloves as they, and not my hands, tore on the gorse and shattered rocks.

We reached the foot of the climb with my body and confidence intact. A walk-in that takes most climbers an hour had taken us 90 minutes; exactly as Martin had predicted. Our speed had picked up after about 20 minutes when Alex had started knocking on the top of the large boulders with the end of his trekking pole to warn me of their position. It was genius, utterly unbidden by me and highly effective as it told me height and position in one as well as giving me a sense of size by dint of the tone the strike made.

As I pulled on my climbing shoes I was delighted to hear Martin say, 'Okay Alex, I'll lead the first couple of pitches. You and Red seem to be communicating well, you can come up with him.'

As this was a circular climb ending up back in the car park we were carrying all our gear in rucksacks, an encumbrance I was unused to climbing with. The first pitch starts with an off-width crack sandwiched between two walls and I *pfaffed* about for a good few minutes trying to get comfortable for the four feet of laybacking it required to get past.

'First move nerves, always happens,' I muttered apologetically to Alex, who had said nothing but now pointed out a knobbly foothold just where I needed one.

'Note to self,' I thought, 'remember to ask for help.'

After that the route seemed to take me in hand and lead me up itself. With Alex a few feet behind occasionally directing me to a better foot placement or keeping me on course with a 'trend left,' I squeezed over the bulges, managed to avoid cracking my head on the low roof and rounded the fine corner to join Martin on the ledge he was belaying from.

Alex joined us and gave me a refresher course on ropeman-ship while Martin led the next pitch. Ten minutes later I felt three tugs on the rope and the distant 'climb!' and I was off again, wriggling round the corner at the end of the ledge that led to a 20 metre tall slab that I romped up.

Martin's belay stance was on a wide grassy ledge. He directed me to a boulder and I began flaking the rope for him.

'Okay?' he asked.

'Oh yes!' I puffed. 'Great rock, it's like climbing buttresses on a church.'

'It's Torridonian sandstone; about 800 million years old and predating any fossil life' he informed me with enthusiasm, and I recalled reading that he had studied geography at university.

By now Alex had joined us and I began paying the rope out as Martin set off again traversing right on little more than a wrinkle in the rock.

'That's where you could feel a bit exposed if you looked down,' Alex said mischievously.

'Just as well I can't see then isn't it' I grinned. 'Don't get scared when I'm gone now.'

It was my turn soon enough. Wind gusted round my feet challenging them not to test the 200-foot drop, but the ledge above my head afforded a degree of security for my hands and I was soon heading upwards across a series of ledges that caused no real challenges except for aggravating my bruised shin.

'Head further left, towards the bottom of the chimney' Alex shouted from below. 'Yes, follow the rope. Don't worry about that cam. I'll take it out.'

He was panting and I realised I was quite far ahead. In the minibus he'd told me this was his first climb in six months after dislocating his shoulder and buggering his rotator cuff. But he seemed to be moving okay and I was feeling very secure on the wall. I looked up to the left and picked out the contrast between the dark scar of a chimney that seemed to rise to the heavens and the lighter rock around it. I climbed to its base, found a comfortable place to bridge and waited for him.

'You know it's hard to keep up with you at times. You wouldn't know you're blind to see you climbing.'

'Ah, well it's a terrific route. So many cracks and flakes to choose from. And having you close by to direct my feet makes life a lot easier. My climbing instructor back in London is always on at me to climb with my feet not my arms but then he's always saying 'not that one, the one next to it and higher'. There's none of that out here. You can even haul yourself up on a bit of friendly heather if you can't find a handhold. It's great!'

I started up the chimney – the kind of climbing I love, wriggling right inside, bridging across and levering myself up on jug-handle holds, letting my back take the weight from my arms my helmet scraping and bumping along the uneven wall behind me. It went up a long way but deposited me a bit like an elevator on the next ledge, beside Martin.

'Brilliant pitch!' I enthused, clipping into the anchor.

'Aye, you did well, good climbing. We're making good time too.'

'I think it's some of the nicest rock I've climbed. Not too abrasive, big responsive holds wherever you need one and a grassy ledge in the sun to relax on at the end of the pitch. I love it!'

'When Tom Patey and Chris Bonington made their first ascent, Patey rolled himself a cigarette here, they all smoked back then, thinking the next pitch looked so tricky Bonington would be ages on it. He'd just lit up when Bonington shouted down telling him to 'Come on up. It's a glorious Diff!''

'I won't get too comfy then,' I promised.

True to form I was soon inching round the end of the ledge and straight into a layback, on my weaker side which was a bit hairy, before pushing out right onto steeper rock that seemed to want to push me further away with every tentative step across its face.

Alex hadn't made a mess of the layback and was right at my heels. 'You're coming to the nasty bulge I told you about. You need to traverse right, step round it then follow the crack up to the next ledge.'

I peered across the traverse and saw the protruding rock outlined against the blue sky, appearing to mark the end of the Earth. It was the same angle as the picture of the solo climber I'd seen on my computer a week before. The small wave of third party vertigo I experienced was the same too.

Alex must have read my discomfort and added encouragingly, 'Nearly there.'

I edged slowly right, swapped feet, felt a thin ledge with my right big toe and worked along it to see whether it widened. It didn't. I got some purchase and went to move my left again. The fingers of my right hand were wedged into a thin crack running at shoulder level, my left gripping a thin flake for dear life. I inched my left foot slowly round in a widening spiral but found nothing.

'Down, left, ten centimetres out, nearly.' I began to wobble, my right toes peeling away. A hand grasped my left, bent the toes gently downward and they met good, firm rock beneath.

'Thanks!' I gasped transferring my weight and shaking life back into first one hand then the other. I found a better foothold for my right and matching hands and feet recommenced the traverse.

Just as I reached the flank of the bulge a cry rang out overhead.

'BELOW!'

Instinctively I pulled myself into the wall, pressing my face against the cold rock, every fibre alert and pumping out the message – 'Don't look up!'

A sharp, grating *'Thunk'* rang out ten feet above and to the left, closer to Alex than me. But impact can send rocks any which way but up and I braced myself as it shrilled towards us.

'Are you all right?'

At times like these you think only of yourself. 'Yes,' I bellowed, to the exclusion of all others.

'Alex?' It was the only occasion I heard anything approaching fear in Martin's voice.

'*Smash!*' The rock exploded into smithereens 300-feet below.

'Fine Dad! That was a big one,' Alex called up.

'As big as a heavy book. I didn't realise it was there and must have knocked it over when I took a step back. I'm sorry.'

'Look Martin, if you don't want to take me up The Old Man of Hoy you've only to say!' I shouted, a late surge of relief hitting me. I'd behaved properly. Twenty-five years after seeing a schoolmate get a face full of pebbles at Harrison's for being too inquisitive, I'd done the right thing instinctively. This was still my element and I was back in it.

The bulge provided no further problems and neither did the vertical crack beyond. I mantled up onto a grassy, boulder-strewn ledge, groped my way past Martin to the anchor sling, clipped in, then let him guide me to a pedestal.

'That lent a frisson of excitement to a Diff,' I smiled.

'I'm just glad you're both okay.' He patted Alex on the shoulder as he passed to the sling then said, 'Right, let's have a break for lunch.'

The packed lunch from the B&B was as good and filling as the breakfast but I made short work of it so stuffed down the majority of a truly minging energy bar that, recalling Matthew's slang term, tasted like soiled sheets and made me gag.

After just half an hour we were on the move again, Alex leading off, giving Martin a chance to watch me over the next couple of pitches. After a bit of a scramble over ledges and boulders we came to a wickedly fun and feature-full crack up the side of a very steep ridge. Martin climbed ahead of me, preferring to give me directions looking down from above. This led of course to confusion between his left and mine. My frustration was compounded by him being a steady, methodical climber, leaving me snapping at his heels and having to rest in places I would not otherwise have chosen.

When I explained that I find it more helpful to have my second directing my feet, because they locate holds less readily than my fingers do, I could sense his discomfort. Expert climbers like Martin feel uneasy underneath amateurs who can be unpredictable and may pull down all sorts of loose material from the face.

All too soon the technical stuff was done and we were scrambling over a succession of false summits and slopes peppered with boulders and the scent of the juniper that grows between them.

'You're a hard man to keep up with, you move so fast,' panted Martin.

'Only on the way up,' I replied, probably the only one of us hoping for another false summit since the walk-off meant another hour of crab-scrambling along the sides of the gully we'd descended earlier.

This however did not dampen my elation at reaching the top. The whole of the West Highlands was laid out at my feet, glorious spring sunshine gleaming from the snow capped peaks and the loch below. Even though the detail was lost on my eyes, the scale and the vivid blues and reds were breathtaking.

'How was that then Red?' Alex's voice contained a warm satisfaction akin to my own.

'That was absolutely brilliant, a terrific afternoon's work.'

'It's looking pretty good for the Old Man of Hoy if you just completed that, I think.'

'If your dad says I can go I'll be there in June. I can't wait.'

'What do you think, Dad?'

'Yes, I think you've proved you'd be up to it. That was a good climb. Well done.'

Alex put his arm round my shoulder and whispered. 'He doesn't say that very often; he means it!'

Agony and ecstasy kept each other in check for the next 60 minutes. Walking off a summit, traversing ground strewn with sharp, shattered rocks wearing climbing slippers is a painful experience at the best of times, but when you can't see what your tightly bunched toes might be about to kick, each dread-filled step registers on a scale of sore to excruciating.

Martin kept my spirits up with a story of an attempted rescue of some sheep from a narrow ledge overlooking the deep gully below.

'These three must have jumped down and were now stuck with no way back to the path. So when the farmer saw me he asked if I could try to bring them up. I roped down and grabbed the first one and carried it up, but as soon as I let it go the stupid thing jumped back down. I tried again but the same thing happened, except this time the sheep missed the ledge. After that I gave up. The other two weren't there the next time I came by.'

In the minibus, my feet throbbing warmly in thermal socks as they expanded to their accustomed volume, I sat back exhausted but elated.

I was going to Hoy ... I was actually going to get a crack at climbing The Old Man and fulfilling a 30-year dream! As Matthew's succinct response to the news put it – 'Fucking A!'

And there was a dollop of icing to come to the cake yet – I still had a day's climbing to go. With the test out of the way we could all relax and have a bit of fun. So Martin took us to a hidden treasure in his own back yard: Diabaig, an outcrop on the shores of Loch Torridon.

It was another idyllic spring day, with a few wispy clouds and a lot of sunshine. Again I had slept well, woken early and, though a little more stiff than the day before and sporting blackened toenails, I felt good and up for a challenge.

We were meeting Nick on the way so had a chance to chat during the drive out. Like me Martin had studied at Cambridge, but spent his spare time cutting holds in the brickwork of disused railway bridges to practice his climbing. He had joined the University Mountaineering Club and used the opportunity to make his first forays to the Alps. Even by his sober and unembellished retelling of it, his ascent of the Eiger a few years afterwards had been an epic that only calm, clear thinking had enabled him and his partner to survive. Nowadays he ran his successful business, led clients on expeditions to his favourite winter and summer climbing regions in-between which he wrote well-received books about his climbs and spent significant, quality time with a family he clearly adored. I warmed to him a lot during those 40 minutes.

'I've been considering how we're going to get you up the Old Man' Martin announced as we bounced down the loch-side road towards the parking area. 'The best way will be for you to climb between the two of us and then, if your friends want, we can take them up the following day. What do you think Nick?'

'Sounds good,' was Nick's typically laid back assessment.

'Um, I think Matthew and Andres were hoping we

could all make the ascent together; you know, all stand at the summit and celebrate the success of a team effort.'

'Mmm. There's nothing to stop them going up by another route and trying to arrive at about the same time, but unless Andres is happy leading E2 then they'd need another guide to go with them. I could arrange that but it would add to the cost.'

'We couldn't go up as a group of five?' Al Alvarez had gone up in a party of six, half of whom were pretty unfit. 'The three of us first with the others following on behind?' That certainly was how I'd read Martin's suggestion that 'one of the guides can climb the Old Man a second time'.

'Large parties tend to move slowly. Besides, Nick and I need to be on either end of your rope throughout, so the others would be fairly much on their own. Unless they're confident climbing at that grade, we can't be worrying about them when we need to concentrate on getting you up safely.'

It was clear that this was non-negotiable and as I digested the information I saw that at its heart lay a concern for my safety. Still it felt like getting a record contract only to be told that the rest of the band was going to be replaced by session musicians. I didn't relish breaking the news to Matthew and Andres.

That however was for another day. More immediate problems lay directly ahead, set in rock with a texture not dissimilar to Yorkshire gritstone. I asked Martin what we were climbing on and he replied with typical precision: 'It's Lewisian gneiss, it's about two billion years old and is the oldest surface rock in Western Europe.'

It didn't feel very nice and I prepared myself for leaving a skin graft somewhere on the crag before the day was out.

The first of the two routes we tackled was *Route Three,* a three pitch E1 that began easily enough with a 4b loosener, before presenting a tricky left to right traverse across a steep, abrasive slab that gave plenty of scope for testing the friction soles of my climbing shoes (much of whose rubber I left behind as tribute to the wall). A thin crack meandered across the face, disappearing periodically, then re-emerging further along, usually where I least wanted it and invariably just out of reach.

Martin kept me on a tight rope but I kept having to ask for slack to allow me to flag further out and grasp the few holds on offer. He couldn't see me from his stance and I was right on the edge of my ability. Had Nick not been there next to me I doubt my nerve would have held. The wisdom of Martin's strategy for Hoy at once became very apparent.

We flopped over the bulging lip of a 60-degree slab, from the rear of which Martin was belaying and I tried to coax my trembling arms and legs back to stillness. Two full-on days of climbing were catching up with me; my shoulders and elbows ached with over-exertion. A bonk bar now would have been a good idea, washed down with a couple of ibuprofen, but all were in my rucksack down below.

'Good effort Red. That was a 5b pitch!' Ever cheerful, Nick wasn't even out of breath.

'It was something else beginning with F too,' I muttered, offering him a Polo.

'The next pitch is easier; it's only a 5a.'

I groaned, 6a on a climbing wall then, I hoped Martin wouldn't climb it too quick, I needed time to flush the lactic acid out of my arms. I stretched them out tentatively then ducked at a cry from above.

'What's that, Martin?' Nick shouted.

'Looks like someone backed off here and left some gear behind. I'm going to see if I can nab it. Looks like a hex and a newish crab.'

'Let me know if it's a 10, I lost one recently and could do with a replacement.'

I was feeling a bit lost until Nick explained that 'hexes' are hexagonal steel nuts, their number denoting their diameter and that 'crab' is slang for karabiner.

Martin was delighted with his trove, 'Good as new!' he shouted down as he clipped it to his harness. Soon enough he was calling 'Off belay' then 'Climb' and I was off again. But the respite had been enough and I attacked the remaining slab and the final steep crack with renewed vigour and the knowledge that painkillers and lunch awaited me back on the ground.

Numbed and replete I knew I had another climb in me but as we ate a chill wind had started to blow, bringing with it the first spots of rain and leaving me worried that we would have to pack up prematurely.

'I think we've got time for one last route before those clouds roll in' declared Martin. 'How about *Dead Mouse Crack*?'

As he set off with a jangle of hexes and cams, Nick observed, 'This one's much more thuggy. It's got a steep corner start followed by an awkward chimney and over-hang out to the right. I think I'll jug up beside you, there's not a lot of room even for one.'

The first thing I did at the foot of the wall was stand in a puddle of brackish water that seeped from a wide, wet, smelly crack.

'Ooh, just like Harrison's,' I remarked. I slithered around a bit, found a deep fissure to lever myself up on and worked my way round the tight corner into what was indeed an awkward chimney, that had me twisting and turning like a pipe-cleaner as I wriggled up beneath the square-cut roof of a jutting overhang.

'You need to emerge front right, round that corner and up.' Nick stood in mid-air ahead of me like some mountaineering genie.

'Marvellous' I muttered. I was back-to-front for the manoeuvre, with two and a half points of contact and slipping.

Contrary to his instructions I buried myself deeper into the back of the chimney. The position allowed me to brace my right leg against the far side of the flue and rest on my left, which was folded under me and toe-hooked into a pocket by my backside.

Twisting my upper body through 150 degrees I groped round the corner till, at full stretch, the fingers of my right hand closed round a solid side-pull. I took a deep breath, swung my right foot across me, round the corner and up, using the momentum to pivot on my left toes and rise to standing. Face hard against the rock now I fought for purchase with my right foot.

'Up, up at hip height there's a ledge.' Nick's voice from above was full of urgency.

I heel-hooked it at the second attempt, dislodging my left in the process. Supported now only by my left hand crimping the corner of the overhang, my left side began to sag. I needed more height to rock over onto my right leg so planted the sole of my left shoe firmly on the abrasive face and tried to smear up on it, groping high overhead for the crack.

'Further out to your right, Red, two more inches. That's it! You'll find a nice deep groove at the back for your fingers. Good. Now pull up!' he urged.

I looped quivering fingers under a lip in the groove and wrenched myself up and past the snout of the overhang, hugging the wall, leaning into its slight angle, wired on adrenalin.

'Well that's one way to do it' Nick grinned. 'Not very orthodox but nonetheless pretty impressive.'

I was on a roll now. The crack above was packed with knobbly holds and chock stones, allowing me to climb up the middle of it on hand and foot jams as I'd learned at Brunel. But all the time the rock was getting steeper and I was getting weaker.

'Last few moves now,' Nick called. 'Go on, nearly there.'

The final few feet bulged out above my head, steep and with no holds apart from the crack. I dropped into a long-reach lay-back and hauled myself arm over arm upwards.

Martin had protected this section well. There was a Friend (a type of cam) embedded in the crack as it ran in from the right to minimise my swing should I fall on the approach, and a medium-sized hex wedged into the base of the overhanging crack. I worked them both out and clipped them to my harness, drew a deep breath and got my feet nice and high to gain maximum height when I pushed up. Another deep breath and I rose, the rock pushing me out and away, my fingers fumbled for purchase in the crack but the rope lay tight in the groove and there were no other holds. I hooked a finger under the rope, grabbed a tuft of heather in my other fist, raised my left leg high and smeared up and over. Just as I felt my balance shift to safety there was a tug at my waist, pulling me back to the void. I slapped my palms down on the rock, friction holding me in check from toppling backwards.

Heart pounding I tried a tentative jerk up, hoping the rope was merely snagged in the crack. Again it tugged me back. My left foot was tucked underneath me, bent like a chicken wing, safely wedged in the crack but the sole bearer of the majority of my weight. The right flailed about for purchase but found little.

'You've got a piece of protection below you, you need to take out' called Nick, also from below.

'Bollocks! It must be stuck under the rope. It's tight in the crack' I called back. It was obvious he couldn't remove it for me unless I came back down again and I felt too pumped and too tired after so much climbing to feel totally confident of getting over again. Equally I had done a lot to exorcise my daemons about overhangs over the past couple of days and was damned if one of them was going to send me home on a low note.

'Do you need a hand, Red?' Nick asked.

'Nah, bugger it. I've come this far; let's get this thing out. Any idea what it is?'

'Another Friend I think.'

I swore. With their spring-loaded open and close action, placing and freeing them is much like depressing a syringe. The problem was finding the end of this syringe to depress. I asked Martin for some slack, wobbled scarily against gravity in spite of my best efforts to hold myself steady, then fumbled between my legs to lift the rope and free the cam.

It was well and truly embedded and I would dearly have loved to see it to work out the angle it had been slipped in at, but I'm used to seeing with my fingers so, with the seconds ticking past and the shakes trembling in my left leg and threatening to dislodge my only solid point of contact, I ran my fingertips along the line of the groove trying to build a mental picture.

Sweat-slick, my right hand began to slip. My left had worked its way along the shaft of the Friend and located the finger grip. I fought to control my breathing and focus only on the job in hand. Nick too was silent. I depressed the bar, felt the cam's teeth close and wiggled the mechanism up and right. It grated all the way then popped out, briefly snagging on the rope before a final yank freed it and I was able to clip it safely to my harness.

Within two minutes I was clambering into a crenellated crow's nest belay stance with Martin, breathlessly telling him of my tribulations five metres below and suffused with a sense of really having achieved something that trumped even my jubilation of the day before.

Martin let me jabber on while he relieved me of the offending ironmongery and its companion pieces before suggesting that it might be time to abseil off.

I felt as if I could float down. Not only had I completed an E1 5b, the same grade as The Old Man, but I'd also conquered a pair of nasty overhangs and kept my nerve and maintained my balance to overcome a problem along the way. If Martin had set out that morning to test my abilities to the limit, he couldn't have chosen a better pair of routes.

I think all three of us left Diabaig more confident that the Old Man lay within my grasp. Certainly we were barely in the minibus before talk turned to press coverage and preserving the event for posterity.

'Alex and I got some good footage of you on the Cioch yesterday and I've taken more today. He's thinking he could pass it to his girlfriend, who's in her final year of a Film and Media course, to make a promotional film with, which would be good for any charity fundraising you were thinking of, and possibly for getting wider interest. I don't know whether you've heard of *The Adventure Show*?'

'It's a rugged Scottish version of *Countryfile* isn't it?'

'That sort of thing I suppose, yes. We've worked with them in the past and Nick's in touch with Meg Wicks, one of the producers. They might be interested in featuring your story.'

I had dropped her an email a month or so before and had a polite, prompt but discouraging reply citing a limited number of programmes and an excess of potential items, but wishing me well for the climb. However with Martin's support, Nick's charm and film footage of me in action to whet her appetite it was certainly worth another try.

'Right, while Nick gets in touch with Meg, I'll go ahead and start booking ferries and accommodation in Stromness. If you can email me with names and final numbers of who will be coming that would be good.'

'Anything else I should do, or work on before June?'

'Your routine sounds good. Just make sure you climb as much as possible and keep up the training.'

With that we shook hands and I climbed into Nick's car to head back to Inverness.

'I'm afraid the B&B I booked you into doesn't do an evening meal but I've been telling Amy about you and she was wondering whether you'd like to join us for supper. It won't be anything special, but she and Lily would really like to meet you.'

My heart leapt. I'd been secretly dreading wandering round an unfamiliar town looking for somewhere to have a meal for one then trying to retrace my steps to the B&B. Also, I genuinely liked Nick, not only was he an excellent climber and intuitive guide but his calm, thoughtful character was full of warmth and humour. I thoroughly looked forward to meeting the wife and daughter he had already described with unselfconscious love and pride.

They were just as charming in reality – both were elfin, with a ready wit and convivial spirit. Over an excellent lasagne washed down with the most-welcome gin and tonic I've ever enjoyed we chatted about books, weddings and the rewards of spending time at home with your children. Amy, who is a GP, and Nick each work part-time so that one of them is always at home for Lily.

I made my excuses after Lily was settled for bed, to leave them some evening to themselves; enjoyed a prolonged shower at my B&B and, when I'd located the bed, fell instantly asleep.

It had been the perfect end to three wonderful days, during which I had fallen in love again with trad climbing and been reminded how much I adored and missed my own family.

Red at Swiss Cottage climbing wall
(PHOTO: MATTHEW WOOTLIFF)

A guiding hand from Matthew
(PHOTO: ANDRES CERVANTES)

Martin leading off Cioch Nose, note the climbing shoes and the rocky ground!
(PHOTO: ALEX MORAN)

Route Three, Diabaig
(PHOTO: MARTIN MORAN)

Crack climbing using the elevator door technique at Latheronwheel
(PHOTO: NICK CARTER)

Red, Keith, Andres & Martin on the ferry to Stromness
(PHOTO: MATTHEW WOOTLIFF)

Hoy's dramatic coastline bathed in perfect evening light, from the ferry
(PHOTO: KEITH PARTRIDGE)

The long walk-in, the Old Man in the distance
(PHOTO: NICK CARTER)

Having got him kitted out for the climb, Red's entourage tries to convince him that the Old Man doesn't look so big... from the promontory
(PHOTO: KEITH PARTRIDGE)

The long and precipitous descent down the cliff
(PHOTO: MATTHEW WOOTLIFF)

450 feet

Pitch 5   80 feet

Final Corner 4b (dihedral)

Pitch 4   115 feet

Exposed Wall 4b

Pitch 3   70 feet

Cracks 4a

The Haven

Pitch 2   80 feet

Overhanging Crack 4c/5a

The Gallery

The Coffin - crux 5b

Traverse 5a

Pitch 1   80 feet

4a

Free-hanging Abseil

25 feet

○ Belays

○ Abseil Points

The Crux Pitch
(PHOTO: KEITH PARTRIDGE)

Opposite: The route
(PHOTO: MIKE LEE, ART: JIM BUCHANAN)

Nick jumaring just above Red
(PHOTO: MARTIN MORAN)

Red exiting The Coffin
(PHOTO: KEITH PARTRIDGE)

Keith and Andres filming the climb
(PHOTO: MATTHEW WOOTLIFF)

It's a long way down and a long way up and it's steep rock all the way
(PHOTO: KEITH PARTRIDGE)

Approaching the sanctuary of the second belay stance
(PHOTO: KEITH PARTRIDGE)

Opposite: A quick rest before the final pitch
(PHOTO: NICK CARTER)

**Near the summit there's a cleft through the rock as if some giant
had taken an axe to the summit**
(PHOTO: KEITH PARTRIDGE)

Rock Gods: Nick, Martin & Red at the summit
(PHOTO: KEITH PARTRIDGE)

Signing the log book at the summit
(PHOTO: NICK CARTER)

Abseiling off – Red and Martin
(PHOTO: KEITH PARTRIDGE)

Opposite: Nick abseiling in mid air
(PHOTO: KEITH PARTRIDGE)

Friends reunited
(PHOTO: NICK CARTER)

Red during cliff-top interview with Keith
(PHOTO: KEITH PARTRIDGE)

13

Down to Earth

'I've always been incapable of accepting fate,
and I've always refused to die, and that has
helped me to survive.'
                                    – Walter Bonatti

The girls were still in Tenerife and the house felt empty,
but a pleasant surprise awaited me when I got home.
Sir Chris Bonington had been in touch, apologising for
the delay, explaining that he'd 'got snowed under with
emails' (an image that made me smile) and finishing: I'm
afraid I haven't got a copy of the BBC film so can't help
you on that one, but the very best of luck on the climb.
Go for it!!!
Chris.

That this message had been sent while I was on the *Cioch
Nose* added a nice note of serendipity. Having the support
of professional mountaineers such as him and Martin
meant a huge amount to me. I wasn't undertaking the
climb as part of some mid-life crisis or publicity stunt but
as a serious challenge to my own damaged abilities and
to the perceptions of others. Had Martin, Nick, Sir Chris
or anyone else in the professional climbing world voiced
doubts as to the wisdom of the attempt or viewed it as a
circus act I would have pulled the plug on it immediately.

'You'll be joining a small elite if you succeed, Red. In fact you'll be forming your own one-man elite as the only blind man to climb the Old Man,' observed my friend Bill, over a pint in the Magdala a few hours later. 'I think it's great. You're looking and sounding better than you have done in years.'

I thanked him and we had another.

'Actually I happened to mention your transformation and its cause to my mum and she told me that her friend Jilly's husband, Brian, was the twelfth person to climb the Old Man, back in 1973 I think she said. He and Jilly went up to Hoy last year and found a little museum there with the original logbook so Brian was able to show Jilly where he'd signed it.'

'I'd love to have a chat with him if he wouldn't mind, the more information on that big overhang I can get the better. Martin and Nick gave me some idea but for them this is a pretty straightforward climb.'

Bill promised he'd see what he could do and we drank more beer. The next day I woke with the first hangover I'd had for months, foreswore ale for the foreseeable future and worried anew about how I was going to break the news to Matthew and Andres that we were not all going to the summit together.

Guilt squatted in my churning guts. I should have fought harder and insisted that, since we were paying, we should get what we wanted. Even as I thought it, that reaction seemed petulant and stupid, ignoring the safety issues at stake. Martin was above all being hired for his expertise.

Still my conscience gnawed at me and I needed little convincing that 'if t'were to be done, t'were best done quickly' if for no other reason than I needed to unburden myself. So I rang Matthew.

'Hey, it's Hampstead's answer to Superman. Have you started wearing your pants outside your climbing trousers yet?'

'Only for paying customers.'

'Well done on getting the OK from Martin. How was it?'

'Absolutely bloody brilliant. Far more fun than I'd dared to hope and the weather was perfect throughout; I didn't need any of that cold weather gear after all but those gloves you lent me were invaluable, thanks.'

'And the radios, how did the three of you get on with them?'

We hadn't. I'd produced them at Moy, only to realise that I had no idea how to set them up. Martin and Nick spent five minutes trying to get them working before giving up and relying on traditional means, which are far more effective in the wilds of Scotland than at the centre of Swiss Cottage roundabout.

'Oh, we didn't really need them,' I said airily. 'I had someone climbing at my feet all the time giving directions.'

'What about communicating when the man belaying can't see you? You'll need them then. I thought the whole idea was for Martin and Nick to get used to using them with you before you climb the Old Man' he persisted.

He was right and the oversight was to have serious repercussions.

'Anyway, Martin was so impressed that he's told Nick to get hold of someone they know on *The Adventure Show*, so we may even get filmed.'

'That's fantastic news!'

'Er yes, fingers crossed. Look there's something else which isn't such great news' I decided to take the plunge. 'Martin is adamant that he wants to take me up alone with Nick and that they will take you and Andres up the following day.'

Silence.

'Yeah, and I've had another look at his email and I think I misunderstood what he meant by him or Nick climbing it twice. I'd assumed he meant one of them would be abseiling down to lead you guys up after me. But rereading it now . . .'

'And I thought the whole idea was to get the three of us standing together at the summit. Look, I'm only doing this so I can see your face when you get there, you know.' It was meant kindly but there was, as I'd feared, a bitter edge of disappointment in his voice. 'Anyway let's discuss this when I get back. I'm in Sardinia at the moment and I've kind of got my hands full. Speak to you soon.'

Bad news delivered with bad timing – I'd really ballsed that up and now felt doubly guilty.

A day or so later I got an email from Jilly confirming that Brian was more than happy for me to ring him one evening, and confiding that his ascent was 'an experience he still dines out on after all these years!'

His voice, like his enthusiasm for climbing, was a product of the Peak District. Both, undiminished by the decades, bubbled over as soon as we came to the subject. He recalled his first bold routes, the minor epics and, most interesting to me, his jaunt to Hoy with his brother and a friend back in 1973.

'We'd all watched *The Big Climb* on TV and fancied giving it a go ourselves. So one Friday afternoon we just decided to pack our gear in the car and drove on up. I don't think we stayed at the hostel but I saw there's one nearby when I was back there last year and when I spoke to the warden he showed me round the museum that's been opened. And there was the old logbook I'd signed all those years ago so I was able to show Jilly my name as proof it really did happen.'

'How was the climb? That overhanging pitch looks a bit of a bugger.'

'I didn't lead that pitch, I'm glad to say. It's a wide crack and a bit loose in places with steep rock above but the holds were there if you went looking, and there was a fair amount of protection left by earlier climbs. Looks like there still is, last year there was even a 150-metre length of rope dangling from the summit.'

'Wow, that must have been one hell of an abseil,' I whistled.

'I'll bet. Yes, it was tough going in places but it's a great climb. The worst bit about it was that we missed the only ferry back to the mainland afterwards, so I was late for work on the Monday and got the sack; but it was worth it!'

By now Matthew was back from his holiday and we arranged our usual Thursday afternoon session with Andres. Cole was at the desk when I got there, slightly early, to return his unworn and undamaged down jacket.

'Hey Red,' his paw enveloped my hand, 'I'm starting to get a little afraid.'

I looked at him blankly.

'For the Old Man of Hoy. Please remember to treat him to respect even as you dominate him. No use reducing the whole stack to rubble!'

News of my success in Scotland had clearly travelled south to Swiss.

'It's all down to your training routine, Cole. Martin was suitably impressed when I described it to him. He does much the same most mornings himself. I would never have had the strength or stamina for the nine hours on the *Cioch Nose* without it. Thank you!'

'Say nothing of it, glad it worked. Just gotta convince Matthew to do the same now.'

Matthew was still carrying his shoulder injury and unwilling to do much more than climb for fear of exacerbating it.

Cole confirmed that I should continue as before, trying to increase the pull-ups by one a week if possible, and incorporating some more back strengthening exercises on press-up days.

'What you really need to concentrate on now is ramping up your climb time. You should be down here climbing twice a week and you need to spend at least one two-hour session a week bouldering. The wall up at Hendon's probably the best place to go. You can train doing traverse circuits round the room.'

'Sounds scintillating' I said without enthusiasm.

'It's usually pretty deserted in the evenings; take Matthew and an iPod. I'll contact the guys there and fix it up for you. Oh and Red?'

'Yes.'

'I think you should buy some new climbing pants, or invest in a belt – we've got rules on decency here.' It was true, I'd lost two inches round the waist and had stomach muscles, which as he'd predicted, pleased Kate no end.

'Unlike our tubby Colombian friend here' Cole announced as Andres sauntered in. 'who's had a whole month back home being fattened up by Mamma.'

Andres puffed out his cheeks, 'Aw God, I have eaten so much and climbed so little. But now I'm gonna quit drinking for the next month and start climbing three times a week because I hear, Mister Red, that we are going to be climbing the Old Man of Hoy together this summer. It's going to be so amazing!'

Clearly not all the news had made it down south.

Matthew didn't raise the subject during the lesson, much of which was spent teasing Andres and exploring the new routes that had been put up in the previous fort-night. One in particular was to prove key to our training.

The holds that you find bolted to climbing walls are moulded to mimic those that you find on different rock surfaces – so you'll get limestone-type holds with small pockets, slopers, pinches etc, and bigger jug handle holds, underclings and sidepulls to resemble the features on sandstone. A good hard route will have a carefully thought out mixture of shapes and sizes set at angles to challenge your balance.

Andres had designed *The Rockover Route* specifically to work on a single technique and he was to have us flog-ging up and down it for the next eight weeks until we'd perfected the skill.

Built on one of the slabs that was at 80 degrees to perpendicular it would have been a cinch to climb on big juggy holds but Andres had used a set that resembled bunches of small red grapes. No single one had more than six bobbles (or grapes) and some had only two. They were widely spaced and the line jagged from side to side, the next hold always just out of reach so that we had to rock over and place all our weight onto one or the other leg to stretch far enough to get to it. This is only possible if you use the other leg as a counter-balance, flagging it out on the opposite side. It was hard, tense work with lots of wobbling and swearing as Matthew and I tried not to fall off tiny toe placements and rise from bent knee to straight leg for the next handhold. I lived in constant fear of my ACLs snapping.

Having avoided discussing the issue of us all summiting together during our lesson, Matthew and I instead arranged to speak over the weekend about the next steps we needed to take. I dreaded the conversation, still feeling I'd betrayed them in some way. This was a team effort. I would never have got this far without Matthew's persistence and Andres' commitment. The three of us should be aiming to celebrate atop the Old Man together.

The problem was, having spent time with Martin and heard his reasoning I could neither fault his logic nor see him changing his mind. I'd also been left with a strong sense that he viewed Matthew and Andres as passengers and I worried that that was exactly how they would be left feeling.

Each month I have put a percentage of my Disability Living Allowance into a savings account, against the eventuality of an unexpected expense, or needing to buy pricey low-vision aids. It had remained untouched for over a decade and as I waited for Matthew's call it occurred to me that it might be well used to repay some of the debt of gratitude I felt towards my friends. It could hardly compensate for the three of us not holding our hands aloft in unison if Martin could not be persuaded to change his mind, but it might help prevent disappointment curdling to resentment.

I kept this to myself however as Matthew and I discussed more practical matters including the kit-list Martin had given me (slings, karabiners, Prusik cords etc.); the possibility of the climb being filmed; publicity and sponsorship. Only as we settled on a division of labour to cover these aspects did the subject come up, and then in rather a roundabout way.

'Thanks for tracking Martin down, Matthew. We couldn't be in better hands. He was clearly gung-ho for the climb by the time I left, and I got the impression he'd given the issues around my sight some thought before I arrived.'

Matthew snorted. 'That's because I rang him the night before you went up and gave him a few pointers on how to get the optimum performance from you. I wasn't convinced he fully appreciated the difficulties you face. It's taken me long enough to understand and I climb with you every week. I wasn't going to tell you but – since we've come to it.'

I could just imagine the mini-lecture. No wonder Martin had been a bit aloof when I'd first got there, then pleasantly amazed after each day's climbing. Perhaps too this was part of the rationale behind having Matthew and Andres climb separately; to avoid too many chiefs fussing round a sole Indian.

'It clearly worked, if only because with such low expectations of me I could only shine.'

'I thought he should know how pissed off you get when it's not going right and how that affects your confidence and ability to listen to instructions. Every week we're effectively trying to achieve the impossible. Andres is trying to climb the wall for you, using his perspective to guide you when that perspective is completely different to yours, partly because he's viewing the problem from down below on the ground and partly because he climbs in a different way to you. And neither of us has any idea how much of what he's saying you're processing anyway, because that's not a constant either.'

I was immediately defensive. 'Well, it's stressful. Put yourself in my position. Most of the time I'm highly uncomfortable, have no idea of what's coming next or when I might rest and half the time I'm being told I've put my hand or foot on a wrong hold. Of course I get a bit short-tempered.'

'It's not criticism, just constructive comment. And you've got to admit it's a fascinating problem. That's why I thought Martin should be aware of it. After all, like I told him, I learn more about myself every time I climb with you. But hey, if you want criticism I can do that too.'

'It's not so fascinating when you're the one clinging to the wall in a stress position' I grumbled. 'Fortunately there's less call for precision on rock, none of this wrong hold business.'

'So run by me again, the reasons why Martin doesn't want us to climb together.' The query came unexpected and caught me off balance.

'Erm, safety reasons mostly, I think. So that he and Nick can give me their full attention and not have to worry about you behind us.'

'And if we climb ahead of you and wait at the top?'

'I don't know. Risk of me getting taken out by falling rocks, I guess. He was pretty adamant that taking you guys up another day was his preferred option.'

'Sure, because that's the one that makes his job easiest. I still think the three of us should be up there together, and I know Andres feels the same. We need to go back to Martin and ask him if there is any way of achieving that. Maybe if we ask one of the guys at Swiss if they could lead me and Andres up.'

'Yes, maybe.' I was doubtful. Much as with Brunel, when Health and Safety and insurers are involved you end up fighting a mechanism that will only grind you down. But since I had so obviously hit it off with Martin the task of going back and arguing the toss with him fell to me.

14

Out-of-Touch and In-Touch

'When I stripped myself completely of pressure
and thoughts of sponsors and realised I only
love to climb, that's the day I did it.'

– Ron Kauk

From the outset Matthew had been adamant that the story
of a blind person attempting Britain's most iconic rock
climb was too good a fundraising opportunity to pass up.
I, however, had reservations that it might look as if I were
using charity to justify undertaking something I wanted
to do anyway – a sort of 'sponsor my mid-life crisis'.

Besides, although I give regularly to a range of charities,
I have a jaundiced view of the bigger end of the sector.
This is in part a result of my dealings with the Royal
National Institute for Blind People (RNIB) – an organisa-
tion dominated by fully sighted professional fundraisers
who appear more concerned about the bottom line than
the blind and partially sighted individuals they are
supposed to represent. They seem to prefer us to stay in
our boxes until such time as we can be usefully employed
as examples of 'people who need your help,' usually when
a fundraising target needs to be met.

Matthew was however both insistent and persuasive
and back in February I had contacted RP Fighting
Blindness, a small charity whose sole mission is to make

111

Retinitis Pigmentosa history. With this end in sight RPFB is funding research into RP gene therapy at the University College London (UCL) Institute of Ophthalmology.

The potential of using gene therapy to treat RP and related retinal dystrophies has been understood for decades and demonstrated repeatedly in laboratory tests. But for that potential to be realised those lab tests need to be refined and proved safe for use on human patients.

As with all diseases there have been many false dawns and miraculous breakthroughs trumpeted for blindness over the years. I have always maintained a healthy skepticism, believing that a cure will be found someday but probably not in my lifetime. Having your hopes repeatedly dashed just adds insult to the welter of injuries sight loss causes. However the speed of recent progress in the fields of gene therapy and stem cell technology (also being investigated at UCL) has made me re-evaluate that view. I now believe that my generation might well be the last to lose its sight to Retinitis Pigmentosa.

Mine is the X-linked variety, passed down the generations in the same way as haemophilia; children of a parent with the faulty gene have a 50-50 chance of inheriting it. Women with the gene are unaffected because they have a spare X chromosome as back-up, but the men develop RP. Both my brother and I have RP and my sister is a carrier, as are my two daughters. We don't know yet whether my nephew has been lucky or unlucky in the genetic lottery.

As far as I'm concerned blindness has become so much part of life that I'm not sure how I'd respond to its absence. I'm not saying I'd refuse gene or stem cell therapy (though I'd prefer not to be one of the guinea pigs) and I'd certainly be grateful if my degeneration could be halted, but I also have concerns about the possible side effects of a cure.

Living with a degenerative disability is psychologically gruelling and requires a degree of acceptance and adoption of the condition that has made my blindness part of me.

I would however not wish RP on anyone, and realise that I am more fortunate in my circumstances than many of my fellow sufferers. Once Matthew pointed out that I had the chance to make a real difference; that in making a little bit of history I could help make RP history; it would have seemed churlish not to raise funds for the Gene Team at UCL.

The Chief Executive of RPFB, was himself planning an assault on Kilimanjaro so was very receptive. Once he'd satisfied himself that I was taking all necessary precautions, he suggested setting up a JustGiving page to publicise 'my challenge,' provide a link to the existing Gene Team appeal and facilitate the collection of overseas donations and Gift Aid. Recognising in me a lack of technological know-how, he offered to set the page up once I'd got the go-ahead from Martin and provided some text and photos.

Not long after my return from Scotland the page was up and running, complete with some excellent action shots taken by Nick and Martin and a truly intimidating photograph of the Old Man itself. I copied the link into an email I'd already prepared and shortly thereafter it began to appear in inboxes everywhere.

£1,000 was donated in the first 24 hours; more than £5,000 by the end of a fortnight! It was humbling to read the messages and know that so many people, some of whom I know well, some hardly at all, some anonymous, all encouraging and supportive, had been so generous in coin and spirit. Matthew had of course been right, and rather than it feeling as if I was using charity to justify the trip of a lifetime, I felt delighted that I was sharing the ride with so many other people.

There was, of course a flipside. I was no longer carrying solely my own expectations, and the question posed by one sponsor 'Do we get our money back if you fall off?' now hung in the background, making me even more determined to succeed.

Momentum began to build, carrying news of my attempt further and wider each day. This was due in no small part to the efforts of another dad from school, illustrator and author Omri Stephenson who designed and maintained a Facebook page for us and kept everyone up-to-date.

With a couple of magazines expressing interest in the story and an interview on BBC Radio 4's *In Touch* programme in the offing, I decided to contact the RNIB. I hoped that they too might view the climb as inspirational and use it to raise awareness, give hope and challenge prejudice. The answer I received shocked even my jaded sensibilities.

'What's in this for us? I'm sure we could do something if you were prepared to give at least a proportion of the funds raised to the RNIB, otherwise we can't really help you.'

It was like my MP demanding cash for questions. 'But, you're supposed to represent all of us; to spread news that may be of interest to blind and partially sighted people, to help us lead independent, fulfilling lives. This isn't just about the money!'

'Why should we help another charity raise funds?'

'Because those funds might help make sight loss a thing of the past for everyone. Because it's in the interests of every blind person you are supposed to want to help!'

This cut no ice. I suppose news of a potential cure threatened her career trajectory. I hope it comes before she, like

114

her predecessor, demonstrates her commitment to blind people by taking a better-paid job at a cancer charity.

Unlike the RNIB, Peter White, the presenter of *In Touch* (and numerous other radio programmes) likes the visually impaired to have a bit of fight in them. Blind from birth, Peter has not allowed others to define the limits of his abilities and has become one of the BBC's most respected broadcasters.

I am grateful to RP for giving me the opportunity to work with Peter and the rest of the *In Touch* team. Since first being invited on to talk about my own book, I have been asked back to review audiobooks, discuss how the new Personal Independence Payments for disabled people will affect me and even been interviewed halfway up a climbing wall!

Far more of my life has been spent listening to BBC Radio than watching TV and I feel a happy sense of belonging whenever I visit Broadcasting House. While I waited in the foyer for Lee Kumutat, the Assistant Producer, and her guide dog Jake, I listened happily as groups of tourists were guided round, soaking up the building's history and proud that snippets of my existence were and would be part of the great BBC archive for generations to come.

Peter was his usual affable self, keen to hear all about the climb and filling the five minutes before we were due in the studio with friendly banter and genuine warmth. His producer Cheryl Gabriel gave me a hug and a glass of water before I settled down in front of the microphone.

As the sound engineer checked our levels Peter reminded me that because of BBC rules he could not advertise who I was raising funds for but would certainly mention that I was doing so.

'Oh, and just to let you know I may ask you whether you'd be happy to keep an audio diary?'

'Er, wow, um, yes okay. So long as the equipment's not too bulky.'

And then we were off.

'Now this time next month visually impaired writer Red Szell will be leaving the relative comfort of his author's desk to tackle what's generally acknowledged to be one of Britain's toughest ascents for a climber. It's the Old Man of Hoy a 450 feet so-called sea stack in the Orkneys. It was first climbed by a team led by Chris Bonington indeed it was a television spectacular and I remember it quite well.

Well, Red is doing it to raise money for research into Retinitis Pigmentosa, the genetic condition which has led to the loss of most of his sight over the years. Only about 2,000 people have ever climbed this. Red started climbing as a schoolboy while his sight was still good, he's now taken up the hobby again and he's determined to take on a climb that has always fascinated him.'

If I'd composed it myself I couldn't have asked for a better, more flattering introduction; Peter really was a consummate host. Feeling quite at home, I waxed lyrical about the documentary that had first turned me on to the Old Man, described what it looked like, gave a brief summary of what the various climbing grades meant and outlined Cole's fitness regime. I had described it to Lee when she'd contacted me about appearing on the programme, but now, hearing Peter's incredulity and Cheryl's low whistle, hoped that listeners wouldn't think I was some kind of body Nazi.

'I think we'll include a clip of you on the climbing wall here,' Peter explained, 'to remind people how you've been honing your rock climbing techniques. So . . .'

So has this all been aimed at climbing the Old Man of Hoy?

It was aimed at getting me back out on fairly serious rock climbs.

I took on the Old Man because my climbing partner Matthew

nagged me into it. I mentioned to him that I wanted to do it one day and he was very taken by the idea, he likes a challenge.

I was delighted I'd succeeded in mentioning Matthew's key role and knew that if a clip from the climbing wall interview was going to be used then Andres and Cole would also appear. After a brief discussion about the technicalities of scaling the Old Man when you can't see what you're doing, Peter asked what he termed 'the naïve question.'

Just how dangerous is it?

I hesitated. My Mum never thought her love of horse-riding dangerous; she knew the risks of course but took precautions against them and enjoyed the ride. It was cancer that caused her premature death. I found myself explaining that I could always be unlucky and get hit by a falling rock or slip and land awkwardly but that I'd be at the end of a rope and everything possible had been done to minimise the danger.

. . . I'm probably more unsafe crossing the Finchley Road.

After the derring-do introduction I'd been given, this must have sounded very glib but Peter was not deterred and tried another tack, asking instead:

What are the most difficult parts of this, technically, for you?

Technically the two most difficult parts are what are called a traverse where I have to move about ten metres from the left down a couple of metres and across a very thin ledge, at which point I'm about 150 feet up with nothing below me apart from the sea and a half-inch wide ledge. A lot of people get very scared at that point because of exposure; you just feel that there's nothing underneath you Fortunately, not being able to see very much, in my own mind I'm only ever five inches off the ground, so I shouldn't imagine that will be too bad. But the bit that really scares me is the overhang, or the Old Man's belly if you like, I have to go up underneath his belly and that sticks out a

*good four to five feet and I don't like hanging upside down and
hauling myself up arm over arm so I'm hoping to get that right
the first time.*

*Now part of this is also to raise money for research into
Retinitis Pigmentosa, the condition that you have. How much
are you hoping to raise?*

That was a surprise. I hadn't expected we'd come back
to the charitable aspect. Good old Peter – *he* wasn't blind
to the wider good that a bit of publicity could achieve. But
I'd been reluctant to set a target figure. Somehow it seemed
grasping when I was delighted just to have people's
support. Put on the spot now I did a quick mental calcula-
tion, reduced it by a quarter, rounded it up and said:

*I'd like to raise £10,000. The JustGiving page has been open
ten days now and so far we're up to four and a half thousand
pounds so fingers crossed we might even go past the target I've
nominally got in my head.*

I was still metaphorically mopping my brow and
wondering whether I'd answered that one well when the
question I'd forgotten about followed hot on its heels.

*With your free hand, how would you like to do an audio diary
for us while you're up there?*

*Urgh ... ah ... you might have to edit out some of the
language. Er ... yes, I will ... um ... happily do so. I hope
you've got a seven-hour tape.*

The interview was over. It had taken barely 15 minutes
that had felt like five. I replayed it in my head and
glugged down another cup of water. Nothing dreadful,
all the main points covered. Lord only knew whether my
guestimate of the summit's area being equivalent to half
a cricket pitch was correct. Peter and the team seemed
happy though and while Cheryl took a few photos for the
webpage, we chatted about my coming back in after the
climb.

With Jake leading us back to the foyer, Lee and I discussed when I should come in to pick up the recording equipment and how much material she wanted me to provide. My main concern was that the device should be as small and easy to use as possible, but I was so thrilled to have been asked that I knew that, even if I were trailing wires, I'd make that audio-diary.

'I don't want you doing anything to put yourself in danger, Red,' Lee insisted, reading my mind. 'We want you back in one piece. If needs be we'll get you back in to do another interview, okay?'

'I promise. My wife would be a bit miffed too if I came back in a box.'

'I'm serious.' Lee's Australian accent, always so mellow on the Radio had acquired an edge that brooked no frivolity.

'I won't take any silly risks, I promise. And, Lee – thank you!'

The interview was broadcast the next evening. Kate, Laura, Meg and I crowded round the radio and I tried not to squirm too much at the sound of my own voice. Only lightly edited it took up over half the show! Peter's small addition closed the piece:

Well let's hope we can get a seven-hour slot for it. And we'll be following Red Szell's adventure later in the summer and there's more details about his climb on our website.'

Within minutes, texts, calls and emails began pouring in. Among the congratulations and flattering comments were a couple of suggestions that I look at my JustGiving page.

There had been a flurry of donations from people who had heard the piece on the radio. Many were blind themselves or former-climbers, or both, wanted to wish me luck and had found my details on the *In Touch* website.

Of all the donations I was to receive perhaps theirs meant the most to me. They felt like an endorsement by people I represented – saying 'good on you, go for it!'

Progress on the visual media front was more mixed, though started brilliantly.

Alex's girlfriend, Pia Agullar Saffirio, had worked long and hard, compiling the clips taken at Applecross and Diabaig and interspersing them with information about the challenge I had set myself. The result was a two-and-a-half minute promotional video that was so good that when she presented it at the Creative Scotland Student Media Festival she won the Best TV Pitch category.

She posted it on YouTube and sent me the link: http://www.youtube.com/watch?v=cc1xkPzoZ-w&feature=youtu.be saying that she hoped it might prove helpful for publicity and fundraising and thanking me for inspiring her in her project! Her film provided a compelling insight into the challenges of climbing blind and proved a hit as soon as it was posted on the Facebook and JustGiving pages.

Unfortunately however the TV production companies didn't bite and Martin's email a few days later was downbeat.

At present it seems unlikely that there will be a professional film team on the climb ... the BBC's production teams haven't expressed any definite interest in actually doing a film. As time is getting quite short I regard it unlikely that anything will happen. We can, of course, all take film on our cameras and put together a good amateur video of the climb in June.

Hope you are keeping in good training.

It was disappointing but everything else was so overwhelmingly positive that I shrugged my permanently aching shoulders and moved on. I was going to get an audio record of the event, which was more my line, and besides I wasn't sure I wanted some TV crew telling me I had to climb that bit again because the light was wrong or whatever!

15

Peak Practice

'Good climbing and good company often go
together. Each is inseparable to the enjoyment
of the other.'
            – Tom Patey, *One Man's Mountains*

A month to go and things on the climbing front were
well on track too. I was up to a full quota of pull-ups,
press-ups, crunches and frencheys and could hang from
each arm for 30 seconds apiece (ten times longer than in
January!) – was it any wonder I felt the call of the wild?

Matthew, Andres and I had a long-overdue date
with Yorkshire gritstone, but busy diaries and wet
weather had stood in our way since my return from the
Highlands at the beginning of April. Time, however,
was now short, and I was itching to get back out on rock
again. Reasoning we'd need at least three weeks for any
sprains, strains or abrasions to heal we moved things
around and found a weekend that most of us (though
sadly not Cole or Trevor) could manage. With great
good fortune it was also a weekend my friend John was
staying in London.

Born and brought up in Buxton, John now lives round
the corner from me. Shortly after his mum was diagnosed
with breast cancer, he had the chance to buy the semi next
door to his parents, meaning he and his young family

could visit regularly without feeling they were crowding his mum and dad.

John senior and I have met many times over the years and shared our thoughts on the cruelty of a disease that has robbed him of his wife and me of my mother. Paying him a visit while we stayed next door in his son's house was not so much a small price to pay for our accommodation, as a pleasure. When he also turned out to be a meteorologist, John senior emerged as the saviour of our weekend.

The weather turned foul the moment we passed Derby, making the Peaks truly dark the closer we got to them. Matthew was driving, an activity that makes him ratty at the best of times and Andres was lolling in the back, fiddling with his iPhone like a hairy, overgrown teenager. With us was Matt Groom, a 26-year-old Special Needs Teacher and part-time instructor at Swiss, who is part of the Rusty Peg crew and climbs regularly with Cole. Slight, agile and calm he possesses all the poise, charm and fair-haired good looks that one associates with a young English gentleman who is also a jobbing actor.

It was Friday night and we arrived in Buxton in time for last orders, so hit the local dive and swilled enough ale to sleep soundly despite the drumming rain. Those of us who woke at 7.00 the next morning took a view and went back to sleep until 10.00, when we were woken by a distinct diminution in the background noise and a hint of colour in the light outside.

Over bacon and eggs Matt checked the guidebook for routes near The Sloth – an enormous overhang with huge jug holds that Cole had recommended as preparation for the Old Man. There was a knock at the back door and John senior appeared.

'Where you off ta t'day lads?'

'The Roaches,' I replied. 'We thought we'd give the Sloth a go.'

John cast a suspicious eye towards the heavens and sucked his teeth. 'Ah don't like look of t'em clouds over there.'

'So long as it stays dry,' I said hopefully.

'A'n reckon it's gonna meet down wi' rain'.

'We'd better get moving then,' Matthew had started to clear the table.

'Bi'ter late, time as got there. It'll be chuckin' it down.'

'Oh it doesn't look that bad.' Matt sounded more hopeful than convinced as he zipped away the guidebook and hoisted his pack. Noises to his left indicated that Andres was shaking salt and pepper onto his sixth slice of bread and remaining resolutely out of the discussion.

'A'n been a me'trologist for fifty-two years now . . .'

'Let's get the kit loaded in the car and get ready to leave in ten minutes,' commanded Matthew.

'Reckon I'll see t'birds before rain starts,' John sighed.

The mist had thickened to light drizzle by the time we parked the car half an hour later. Andres shivered as he stepped round to the boot.

'I would have thought you'd got used to this when you were studying in Manchester,' Matthew teased.

'I will never get used to this shit weather. Why is it always so cold and wet in this country?'

Laden with ropes and racks we trudged up past Don Whillans' hut and sloshed through muddy puddles towards the Upper Tier, only to be driven under cover by a strafing of heavy raindrops.

'Looks like Old John was right after all,' Matthew muttered.

Matt had the guidebook out and was flicking through pages. 'Ah, thought so. *Raven Rock Gully*. It's only a Diff but it's sheltered. We might as well warm up on it till this rain clears. '

It was basically a cave with a chimney and dripped with watery green slime. But it was out of the main squall and, with careful placement most of our gear could be hidden under overhangs and at the back of ledges.

A low moan rose from the edge of the cave. 'Aw shit, no, I don't believe I've done this thing! I am such an idiot!'

Andres, it turned out, kept two identical climbing bags; one with his bouldering gear in; the other, the one he had just discovered he had left behind, with his harness, helmet and slings needed for tackling anything over ten feet tall.

'I am such an asshole!' he wailed.

Matthew was inclined to agree. 'You complete Muppet! You're meant to be in charge. Didn't Uncle Cole pack for you?'

'I've got plenty of chalk.' Andres held out two bulging chalk bags.

'Oh that's useful, I'll know who to ask if I can't get any grip on this gritstone!' Matthew said witheringly.

'Do you know how to make a harness from slings?' Matt interjected.

Andres had his iPhone out in a trice and was soon consulting the UK Climbing website. With Matthew still chuntering about some people being more focussed on remembering their hair gel than their harness, Andres cobbled together the necessary items from our kitbags and soon stood before us rigged up in a white saltire arrangement.

'I look like such an asshole,' he moaned, glancing about to check there were no other climbers in sight.

'Serves you right. Maybe next time you'll actually

check you've got the right kit before you arrive' Matthew snapped.

Matt led off, giving a quiet running commentary as he went. I was next up. It wasn't difficult; the cracks were wide, the gradient slabby, requiring plenty of bridging. But it was slippery as hell, the only example of frictionless gritstone I've ever come across. I thrutched my way up, keen for an early, confidence-boosting success. The walls closed in with every move and the phrase 'rat up a drain-pipe' played round my head on continuous loop.

'It's a little awkward at the top,' Matt shouted down, 'The exit's through a sort of manhole but you need to turn through 180 degrees first then push yourself out head-first.'

'Sounds like being born,' I panted. I did as I was told and plopped out by his feet, into a howling gale.

Andres followed, grunting up a passage that was far more narrow for him than me and moaning that the slings cut into his 'Queen's Jewels'.

'I wonder if his shoulders will fit through the cervix,' I mused as a particularly loud groan echoed up towards us.

Finally though, with some effort and a bit of tugging, he too flopped onto the belay stance where, five minutes later, we were joined by a highly critical Matthew.

'That was the most disgusting, stinking, wet route I've ever climbed. I suggest we find something nicer to climb next.'

'I don't think we'll be climbing anything for a bit. I don't like the look of those dark clouds over there.'

'You sound like John senior,' Matthew said, following Matt's nod to the south. 'But I think you may be right.'

'We packed up the gear and slithered back down the path to the car, getting most of the way before the sky darkened and deposited its load on us.

We got a further hosing on the short sprint across the Roaches Café car park before taking shelter and solace in tea and cake, and introduced Andres to the joys of custard.

An hour later there was still no let up and, having consulted the café owner who was happily restocking his display, we decided to call it a day with just one exceedingly scruffy 20m Diff to our names.

Back at the house John senior popped his head round the door to find what success we'd had.

'Aye, it'won't be dry again a' t'Roaches today.'

Andres sighed loudly and wandered off to watch TV. Matthew was more diplomatic. 'Where would you suggest we go?'

John senior cast a weather eye across the steaming roof of his canary coop and sucked at his teeth.

'Th' might try Castle Naze. Reckon you might get a coupl'a hours bifore clouds come over and it starts chuckin it down there too.'

Matt immediately began leafing through the guidebook to identify possible routes while Matthew and I chatted with John about the Cup Final being played that afternoon and the delights of the English weather.

Following John's precise directions we found the crag easily enough, placed ourselves out of the cold gusting wind and enjoyed two hours of grunty abrasive climbing on an intermittently sunny south-facing wall that was rich in Hard Severe routes and an E1 5C called *Pod Crack* (which we all fell off).

Matt was shivering when I joined him at his windswept belay stance at the summit of what proved to be our final ascent of the afternoon.

'You better tell the others to pack the gear quickly and head down to the car. I'll get the top rope and join you there. Did you get all the protection?'

I confirmed I had and asked why.

'That' he replied ominously, 'unless I am mistaken, looks like a hailstorm. I reckon we've got about 20 minutes.'

I followed his arm and even my dim eyes could see a teeming black mass spread across the horizon, as if a plague of flies had risen. I abseiled down as quickly as I could and relayed the news.

Matthew sprang into immediate action, ramming equipment into bags and finding my boots and stick for me. Andres seemed more intent on fiddling out a red LED that someone had slid into a fissure to mark a night-climb route. We left him to his crack booty and set off down the hill, Matthew as ever leading, me a step behind with my hand on his shoulder for guidance, like a section of the human chain of First World War soldiers blinded by gas and filmed trudging to safety across Flanders mud.

The battery from above opened up when we were still 20 metres from the car. Hailstones bombarded us as we slithered over the stile and into the shelter of the Volvo. It was so dark Matthew had trouble tracking the others fleeing downhill to join us.

Nobody noticed the four steaming strangers who stumbled into the Beehive Inn ten minutes later. As we opened the door Wigan scored a last gasp goal to win the FA Cup. The partisan crowd clearly had no links with the City side of nearby Manchester and there was jubilant uproar.

'At least it's pissing down in London too' observed Matthew as we savoured our beer and discussed plans for the following day, which we agreed should be passed by our weather expert before being finalised.

Conditions at breakfast time Sunday morning appeared, like Andres' hair, perfect. John senior joined us again as we were checking ropes and protection and we ran our plan past him.

'Well you've come to t' right man. A've bin a me'trologist for fifty-two years now, so I reckon I should know thing or two 'bout t' weather' he reminded us.

'You were spot on yesterday,' I acknowledged.

After some gentle admonishment not to be taken in by the sun and warmth streaming through the kitchen window, John gave his ruling. 'A'n reckon t'won't star't rain over Roaches bifor lunch time.'

We thanked him profusely and I stayed chatting with him while the others loaded all our kit in the car and made ready to leave. Finally it appeared that the Sloth might lie in our sights.

The Upper and Lower Tiers of the Roaches looked far less welcoming than Buxton's warm limestone, but the previous day's howling wind had subsided into a low moan and the sun was even making a tentative effort to appear. Other climbers were out which was an encouraging sign though their reaction to seeing me being led up the broken path, white stick in one hand, Matthew's shoulder in the other, left a little to be desired.

'Fookin' 'ell' one muttered to his mate as we passed 'it's a blind man an' tha' lot's tekkin' 'im climin'!'

'Yeah, blind not deaf,' I growled back.

Access to the Sloth and much of the Upper Tier was barred by miserable looking men in day-glo orange who looked like they should be marshalling an orienteering exercise but were in fact protecting some peregrine falcons who had chosen to breed out of reach of all but the most agile nest robbers. Grumbling about Nature taking precedence over the Ascent of Man we trudged away to set up camp further along. We were soon joined by the pair of climbers we had passed earlier, plainly keen to see the limits of blind ambition.

They had all the gear – expensive jackets, shiny cams

and nuts jangling above suspiciously clean climbing shoes – and set up at the foot of *Sparkle*, an 8m HS 4b that culminates in a burly overhanging bulge that you can climb round and over in the orthodox manner or take direct with a ballsy HVS 5a move. Its silhouette didn't look pretty from below.

Neither did our two locals as they attempted to scale it. As we shuttled up and down a nearby flakey, pock-marked Severe 4b warmer-upper, they grunted and swore and repeatedly failed to get higher than halfway. At least, remarked Matt, they were putting a few scratches on their gear even if they had no idea of how to use it.

Once they had abandoned their attempt and wandered off to something less vertical but within spying distance, we took their place. Matt led off, and made a graceful, almost effortless ascent, only struggling at the topmost bulge, which on second thoughts he took round the side.

Next it was Matthew. He made a bit of a cod's of the traverse from the first to the second slab and took the less technical approach to the bulge but climbed the route very well.

Andres made a typically feisty assault, coming a cropper on the lower section as a result, but otherwise powered up and over, rather like a tank through a forest.

I stood disconsolate waiting for the tugs on the rope to signal Matt was ready to belay me. It was Brunel all over again. The others had done the overhang; it only remained for me to prove my mettle. And I had an audience.

The flake rising about ten feet from the base required a left-sided layback – never my strongest move. I peeled off twice and imagined I could hear muffled chortling from Sheffield-way. The third time angry determination got me up to the ledge above. Matthew read the signs and urged me to take a rest. After that the traverse to the second slab, the wriggle up a wide-ish crack and the move to the ledge below the bulge weren't too troublesome. Only when Andres who had walked down from the top, began shouting encouragement and directions, muddling left and right and sending me off the end of the ledge, did things go wrong again. Cursing, I regained my stance and politely requested that he 'shut the fuck up and let me work it out for myself.'

The fat bulge pushed into my face and chest as I edged gingerly out along the narrow ledge, groping for the handhold that I knew from the others lay somewhere far out on the left at shoulder height. When I'd pushed my left foot out as far as I dared and still found nothing, I flagged with my right to gain extra reach. Now one of only two points of supporting contact, the fingers of my right hand that were wedged into a razor sharp crack above began to go numb.

Finally my left index and middle fingers hooked a side-pull. Rocking slightly further over on my left leg I found I could close the majority of my hand round it and was able to wriggle back into balance.

Everyone down below was very quiet; holding their breath.

Direct route or bypass? Whatever I decided, I needed a bit of height to judge what lay above. So, groping around, first with my right foot, I located a beautifully solid edge at knee height, then my right hand too found a 'thank God' hold. Hoping that I wasn't too far shy of the summit and that it was more ledge than bulge, I thought 'bollocks, why not?' and pushed myself up, round and over.

Jamming my left knee under the overhang I launched my left hand high overhead then ran it down the rock face till it snagged in a crack. Wedging my fingers deep inside, I levered up against the friction tugging at my jacket. My right foot found purchase on something and I got my right hand up and over the top of the bulge where it discovered . . . smooth rock! Breathing hard I had a tense few seconds as my fingers scurried around for something to grab before locking into a tiny divot. I rose shakily to standing. The skin on my left hand tore in a dozen places as I forced it up the crack and out onto the smooth, weathered ledge where it found first Matt's boot, then the tangle of rope and finally a tussock of wiry grass. One last heave and I was over!

'Nice one Red. Very bold!' Matt grinned, directing me past him. 'That was really strong climbing!' Below, I heard cheering.

'I think you did that better than any of us,' remarked Matthew on my return to terra-flatter. 'And I got some great pictures of your backside for you to show your wife!'

By now our local neighbours had slipped away, we hoped with chagrin rather than a presentiment of rain. We worked our way along the Upper Tier to the base of *Calcutta Crack,* an HS 4b described as '6m. The twisting crack is very tricky, especially for the short.' Though I was walking tall I remained concerned by the observation.

'Jesus Red. You can't climb with your shoes in that state, they're covered in sheep shit.' Matthew grabbed a towel and began scraping at the soles of my climbing slippers. 'The things I find myself doing for you' he muttered. 'If you'd told me I'd be doing this . . .'

'I've always wanted a batman; like Lord Peter Wimsey or Albert Campion. So are you a Bunter or a Lug, Matthew?'

'I haven't a clue what you're talking about but you can piss off if you don't want to wipe shit off your own shoes.'

The mood had lightened now we'd got some routes under our belts and though the sky to the South had turned ominously grey Matt reckoned we had time for this last one.

It was a feisty little number that packed a lot into its six metres and provided good technical practice. But the first plops of rain were spattering us as Matthew led me down the winding, slabby path to the base again and we packed quickly and decided to call it a day.

Perversely the sun broke through just as we passed Don Whillans' hut again, allowing the other three to enjoy a quick 20 minutes bouldering before the clouds crashed shut and we knew another storm was on its way.

It had been a frustrating but ultimately fun weekend with plenty of beer and laughs and just enough climbing to leave us all feeling satisfied. At times it had been a bit tense, mostly due to elements beyond our control. Some of Matthew's comments had been a bit near the knuckle but no one had taken offence.

Somewhere south of Derby Matt asked whether I had any Stone Roses on my iPod – he was thinking of going to see a film about them but didn't really know their music. As Matthew and I sang along to *Waterfall* and *She Bangs The Drums* we reminisced about what we'd been getting up to in 1989.

Andres looked up from his iPod and announced; 'Hey guys, that is so long ago. You know, I was three years old.'

'It's still good though!' Matt added.

I calculated that he could only have been two when the album was released and a small wave of sadness lapped round me bringing with it realisation. Matthew and I were old enough to be fathers to these two. No doubt much of the tetchiness Matthew had shown with Andres in particular was born of having a teenage daughter who manifested much of the same insouciant behaviour. The added layer of responsibility he clearly felt for me too can have done little for his stress levels. Climbing is not a dangerous pastime until one of the team takes their eye off the ball and makes a careless mistake – then it can be fatal. The trouble with young climbers is that they often appear to be too laid-back, even lackadaisical – the antithesis to Matthew's thoroughness.

The opening chords of *Made of Stone* came blaring out of the car stereo and we all began to sing along to a song we recognised. I put my worries aside. Notwithstanding the sometimes-bumpy walk-in, the four of us had enjoyed climbing together and were driving south having proved Tom Patey's assertion, to a sceptical audience: 'The word impossible has no permanent place in a climber's vocabulary.'

16

Buffing Up

'I say the last 10% of the way to perfection
takes so much of your life that it isn't worth the
effort. This overzealous attitude is what creates
religious fanatics, body Nazis, and athletes who
are exceedingly dull to converse with.'

– Yvon Chouinard

The weather changed and all the seeds we'd planted
during the previous months, fed by the endless rain,
began to erupt into bloom. Over the next four weeks the
project seemed to take on a life of its own, leaving me to
concentrate on being physically and mentally prepared,
and enjoying the sunshine.

From the moment I returned to London, friends and
neighbours quizzed me on how our trip to the Peak District
had gone, wincing at the sight of my hands (which looked
like they'd been through a meat grinder) and, convinced
by such a raw statement of intent, spreading the word.
Sponsorship and good wishes flowed in. John Weston
junior's message on the JustGiving page was typical of
their generosity:

'A Gherkin-high rock, over the sea, 'in a blindfold'; that
raises the bar; the next to ask me for marathon sponsorship better be doing it on their hands!'

With the broadcast of *In Touch* bringing an even wider

audience I was contacted by the editor of *Grough,* an online magazine that provides 'the inside view of the outdoors'. He wrote a terrific, eye-catching article about my attempt, which in turn was picked up by *Times Scotland.*

'Hey man, you're going' viral. There's even a UKC forum opened up about you!' Cole's laconic Southern drawl was almost tinged with excitement. 'And Christmas has come early for you this year.' He plonked a box on the table beside me, and flipped open the lid.

Spurred on by Matthew, I had asked Cole whether there was any chance that Mammut, the Swiss Alpine equipment retailer who have concessions at many High Sports and Climb London walls, might sponsor us with some of the gear we needed. Ever supportive, Cole promised to have a word in the relevant ears and I'd given him a shopping list.

Christmas had indeed come early! I pulled out a lightweight wind and shower-proof jacket, a summer fleece, climbing trousers, karabiners, a new belay plate, a packet of slings for every eventuality and a really natty 12.5 litre daypack. They had also let me have a 60-metre rope at cost price, for future expeditions.

'If you could try to get a couple of photos of you climbing in their gear, Mammut would be very appreciative' Cole added, 'but otherwise they just said to wish you good luck.'

I was ecstatic. Quality climbing gear is far from cheap and my budget was running close to capacity, especially since I had decided to foot the bill for all three of us.

A further discussion with Martin about hiring a guide to lead Matthew and Andres up the *South Face* route had ended with Martin's assertion that coordinating two parties to summit simultaneously was problematic and the location inhospitable. I suppose I could have argued the toss with him but suspect it would have achieved little, save to make it look like I was questioning his professional judgement.

There would be no photograph of the three of us celebrating atop the Old Man of Hoy together. Matthew and Andres were of course disappointed (as was I) and Matthew was even more peeved to find that Mammut had only supplied me with gear. Some light relief was provided by the fact that I'd ordered the trousers when my waist had been three inches stouter so that they fell down to my ankles when I tried them on, but there was a slight edge to his comment: 'Well, I suppose you *are* the star of the show.'

Fortunately he is not one to hold a grudge, which was just as well as we were spending an increasing amount of time together. We'd done a couple of evenings bouldering at Hendon before going to the Peak District but now ramped up to a two-and-a-half hour session each Wednesday.

Typically we'd arrive at 8.00 pm, me with my iPod, him with a portable speaker, and listen to something loud and rocky as we did 20-minute circuits round the four walls of a tennis court-sized, windowless room. It was stifling, sweaty and unforgiving when you slipped and fell. What the poor staff there thought of two middle-aged men stripped to the waist, listening to the King Blues or Depeche Mode and stuffing their faces with chocolate between traverses, god only knows! But it was bloody good fun and helped cement a growing friendship.

We were also beginning to teach each other techniques that we had gleaned from climbing DVDs such as Neil Gresham's *Masterclass* and perfecting skills that Andres had been working on with us. He meanwhile was climbing during his breaks at Swiss and spending his evenings on a bouldering wall in Bermondsey.

I was feeling strong and positive. Even my fear of injury had receded and I allowed myself off the leash a little. I kept up with the training programme and climbed at every opportunity but was no longer so quick to turn down going out for a drink or a curry. The trip to the Peaks had reminded me of the camaraderie of a night out with the lads. Plenty of friends wanted to take me for a final few pints before I risked life and limb on Hoy; many had barely seen me over my six abstemious months. Consequently the last couple of pounds I'd planned to lose, to take me to my target weight of 10½ stone, went on rather than coming off.

I wasn't the only one. Andres and Matthew were also dining out on the buzz surrounding the climb. Our weekly sessions at Swiss, during which we were regularly tackling 6a+s and 6bs, often had a febrile quality born of pushing ourselves to our limits on not quite enough sleep and a mild hangover. We'd done the hard work now and were under starter's orders, ready to go.

Only two thistles remained in a garden that was otherwise rosy. The first was my continuing struggle to find the right climbing shoes. Having taken Cole's and Andres' advice I had invested in a pair of Scarpa Vantages, an Italian lace-up shoe with a slim fit, reasonably pointed toe and good, solid rubber edge to the sole. They were mid-price and known to be relatively durable; and had been perfect for the three months they'd lasted.

Because I explore the wall as much with my feet as my hands they, like every other pair of climbing slippers I've owned, wore rapidly through at the big toe. When I went to order a new pair I found that Vantages had been discontinued. One pair remained at a shop in Covent

Garden so I reserved them and hotfooted it down there. Having size 8½ feet I ordered 7½ shoes. They felt a bit tight when I tried them on but I was in a hurry to get to Swiss so grabbed and dashed.

After an hour of climbing my feet felt even more like they'd been in a vice than usual. Matthew checked the box – US 7½, UK 6½! The salesperson, I remembered now, had a stateside accent; no wonder the assistant I'd paid had remarked that I clearly preferred an aggressive shoe! Fortunately, being end of the line, they'd been half price – because now they were too worn to return.

I kept them for tough, single pitch routes, rang the shop again and, making sure to quote the EU size, asked whether they had any in stock. After a bit of searching the final pair in the country was located, in its Bristol store. They could be sent to Covent Garden and would be ready for collection in a fortnight.

Two weeks of climbing in the 6½s did little for the sensitivity of my feet but they still informed me that something was amiss when I tried this latest pair. They were both the right size but unfortunately they were also both the right foot. The sales assistant seemed a little put out, reminding me that they had gone to some trouble to obtain them for me. Over the next hour I tried every climbing shoe in the shop and finally, with some desperation, settled on a pair that felt almost fine.

Cole made a teeth-kissing noise when he saw them. 'Nice colour. Though Red Chili have a poor reputation for quality.'

I was already pushing my luck buying new shoes so close to a big climb – I didn't want to take blisters to Hoy. They'd last long enough. That assumption was however destructively tested by a combination of my foot-groping technique and Yorkshire gritstone. By the time I got back to Swiss my big toe was already feeling more through the thinning leather than it wanted. With only four weeks to go there was no time to wear-in a new pair even if I did manage to get a refund (which was doubtful). All I could do was treat my red shoes gently, alternate them with my aggressive baby shoes and hope.

The other thistle was the nagging concern that I was making a claim that I could not be 100% sure of. I had checked with both UK Climbing and the British Mountaineering Council that they knew of no other climbers who had logged a first blind ascent of the Old Man. The two obvious candidates, Erik Wiehenmayer and Gerrard Gosens, certainly hadn't and when I'd quizzed Martin, who was about as great an authority on the Old Man as I was likely to find, he'd known of no other attempts. But with news spreading far and wide, I had to prepare myself for the eventuality.

So my heart fell when I read the following message attached to a JustGiving donation from a guy called Steve Bate:

Hi Red, I'm a climber with RP. Good luck. I'm going to Yosemite to climb, give me a mail through my Facebook page Visual Aid – Climb Zodiac.

I checked the page and did a little digging around on the Web and discovered that Steve was a seriously talented climber who was proposing to become the first blind man to solo-climb El Capitan! Not only that but, until his diagnosis a couple of years earlier, he'd been working as an instructor in Scotland. All of which increased the likelihood that he may have beaten me to it.

I hadn't set out with the intention of breaking new ground; I'd just wanted to climb the stack that had seduced me so many years ago. But what with the charity fundraising and the need for a strapline to advertise my attempt, 'Red Szell aims to become the first blind man to climb the Old Man' had become enmeshed in the project. Now, fearing I had made a false claim, I typed my message to Steve with trepidation.

His reply not only set my mind at rest but offered me the one thing I realised I had hitherto been lacking – someone who knew exactly what the challenges were because he faced them too; a one-man peer group.

Hi Red,

A friend of mine sent me a link to your radio 4 interview which I listened to yesterday. That's awesome what you're doing. I think my friend Alex climbed with you on the Cioch Nose and he was really impressed and thinks you will cruise the Old Man. I too have RP and do a bit of climbing. I was diagnosed two years ago and that shook my life up for a bit making it all new and unknown for a while. I currently have a 10-degree visual field which I think is a bit better than your vision from what Alex told me. It's a shame I didn't find out about your trip earlier as it would have been great to climb with you. I'm a mountaineering instructor and have led people up routes for a few years now.

I'm about to head out to Yosemite to try and Solo a route called Zodiac on El Cap. I think the route is going to take 10 days to climb and going to be a real big challenge. Like yourself I've been training for a year and it's only in the last few days I have felt fit and not tired all the time.

I've never climbed the Old Man but I have climbed the Old Man of Stoer a couple of times and Am Buachaille off Sandwood Bay the other two famous stacks behind Hoy. Both of those were really good adventures and I really enjoyed those routes. I'm away until the end of June but I very much look forward to hearing about your adventure on my return, and maybe we could share a rope one day in a joint effort to raise more funds. I'm trying to raise 5k for a local charity that have helped me come to terms with RP. I'm also a member of RP Fighting Blindness which I'm surprised they didn't put us in contact as I called them to let them know what I was doing.

If you have any media contacts that you think would be of use to raise awareness of RP that I could contact before I leave that would be much appreciated.

If you have time to give me a call it would be great to talk to you. If not I wish you the very best and I'm sure you will enjoy the adventure. It's great to know there are others out there like me still pushing hard to live their dreams.

Cheers Red

Steve

So this was the guy who Alex Moran had been talking about the day we'd climbed together. He hadn't mentioned El Cap though. Solo aid climbing is about as hardcore as it gets. The climber has no partner to follow him and remove his protection, so has to rappel back down and do so himself, effectively climbing the wall twice, and he takes all his equipment (bedding, food and water) with him; dragging it up behind him on a rope. El Cap is 1000m high and Steve was hoping to do it in ten days, which meant carrying sixty litres (60 kg) of water alone!

He was in good hands though, a good friend of Paralympic cyclist Karen Darke, he was going out to Yosemite to acclimatize with her partner and El Cap guru, Andy Kirkpatrick.

We chatted happily for the best part of an hour, Steve's chilled out Kiwi accent making light of what must have been a brutal couple of years both in terms of his diagnosis, loss of his driving licence and career and his adoption of a punishing fitness regime that I suspected put the Cole Styron Workout in the shade. Steve too had a supportive wife and friends and told me that rather than getting all mawkish about his loss of sight, Karen's reaction had been; 'Great, we could do with you on the British Paralympic team!'

We arranged to keep each other posted on our progress and I put the phone down knowing I had banished another aspect of the desolation that lurks in the wings when you have a disease that gradually cuts you off from the world.

The final fortnight before our departure began with an interview in the local newspaper *The Ham & High* complete with vertigo-inducing photos of me, taken from above on *The Cioch Nose*, that brought gasps from neighbours and a renewed flurry of activity on the donations front. Chief among these were the East German Ladies Swimming Team, many of whom I had met at Al Alvarez's book launch. Even these hardened year-round outdoor bathers were impressed by what they'd seen and read and were extremely generous in their sponsorship. One even made the following bizarre pledge: If Matthew climbs in his Speedos I'll double the donation!

Another unexpected surprise came in the form of a DVD posted to me by a well-wisher who had heard of my difficulty in finding a copy of *The Big Climb*. Somehow he had managed to track down the first episode and burned me a disc. Watching it was as much a history lesson as a guide to the route. The grainy black and white footage and ponderous long-shot camera work suited my eyesight very well and reminded me of episodes of *Z-Cars* when I was growing up. I got a very good sense of the scale of the task ahead and a pretty good look at the overhang. They were all there including Joe Brown, making steady, elegant progress up seemingly impossible rock; Tom Patey, always quick with a witty remark; and Chris Bonington, resplendent in woolly climbing socks and what looked like breeches.

With Chris Brasher of the BBC providing and receiving running commentaries via a two-way radio system, I watched closely as the six climbers toiled up their three chosen routes, Bonington and Patey on the original *East Route* that I would be taking. I took careful note of how they stopped regularly to brush away what Bonington called 'a kind of thin slime of wet sand that's just like ball-bearings' from each ledge, so that they could get purchase. As Bonington entered the bottom of the big chimney crack that leads to the overhang I sat on the edge of my seat, intent on gleaning any knowledge I could.

The audio drifted in and out of range as he worked his way deep into the Old Man's innards from where odd phrases like: *'it starts getting really awkward going . . . hand-jams deep in the crack, it's a real grunt . . . it gets pretty desperate . . .'* emerged periodically.

Brasher: *This is the sort of situation where somebody who wasn't quite so good would get into real trouble.*

Bonington: *If I did fall off here I'd go about fifteen to twenty feet clear of Tom and it would be a hell of a job to get back in again . . . My wretched crash hat is too big to fit in the chimney . . . It's very slippery . . .*

I leant forward, keen to see how he worked his way out from under the overhang to a position where he could gain purchase. At that moment the BBC, in its infinite wisdom, cut the team on the arête. I sat back swearing at the TV.

Five minutes later we were back with Bonington. He had got his head clear and was bridged one foot on either side of the bottomless crack, 150 feet above the waves and not looking particularly comfortable. Brasher asked him how he was getting on.

Bonington: *This is a particularly awkward one. You've got to get right, straddled out.*

Brasher: *Your right foot doesn't look as if it's on much.*

Bonington: *It's my left foot actually is the worse one; the right isn't too bad. The worst thing is there's nothing for holds up here to speak of and you've just got to press on. I'm pressing on my right arm and just balancing up. I'm now getting my right foot up. I'll get a bit further up the crack and then I think I'll be able to get out right out onto the edge. Another straddling move, it's straddling all the way just here, it's er . . . a bit awkward . . .*

This was it, the crux move; how to escape from the overhanging, bottomless crack they call the Coffin and I was about to see it done by the expert. I was on the edge of my seat.

Bonington: *I'm now going to reach right up here to try and get my left foot up . . .*

Brasher: *Can we go to Joe Brown? I'll shut Chris Bonington up.*

I hurled abuse at a man long dead for actions that had occurred before my birth. By the time they cut back to the East Face Bonington was safely installed on his belay ledge and Tom Patey was hanging beneath the overhang, fag in mouth and fixing Jumars.

Patey: *When I launch out into space here just now, you'll have some idea just quite how steep this pitch is.*

Kate, Laura and Megan all gasped as he swung out to reveal just what would be facing me in a few days.

'That's huge! Seriously Dad, how are you going to do that?' Laura, who gets vertigo at anything over seven metres, and who had already pointed out just how tiny

145

the six figures crawling up the Old Man looked, sounded genuinely worried.

'He can always use those clampy things like that man is,' Meg replied defensively. Ten years old and slightly built, she is a fearless and determined climber at Swiss who had begged me to take her climbing outdoors. However when, halfway through the DVD, I'd jokingly suggested she come to Hoy with us, she'd merely shaken her head in mute astonishment at the scale of what she was seeing.

Kate was keeping her thoughts to herself. That morning she'd rung to say there had been a British man killed on El Cap, and that she hoped it wasn't Steve (it wasn't). Over the next fortnight two more Brits were killed by rockfalls there and two climbers, one of them known to the guys at Swiss, died on Anglesey. My glib assertions that I was less safe crossing Finchley Road and that the majority of climbing fatalities occur in winter conditions, were beginning to look as crumbly as the lower reaches of the Old Man.

And all the time the weather in The Highlands and Islands remained windy and wet; ensuring that, if I got to climb at all, those ball bearings would be slippery as hell.

Safety concerns were at the forefront of Lee's mind when I met her at the BBC Production Equipment Centre. She'd had to fill out a gargantuan risk assessment document and made me promise again that I would abandon the recording should it become an encumbrance.

The MP3 recorder itself was ideal; big chunky buttons, white-on-black display and so simple even I could operate it after a minute's tuition. The technician assured me it had ample battery life but gave me a box of AAs just in case. I was about to leave when he handed me the headphones and mike.

'I can't wear these cans – they'll never fit under my

helmet!' I protested. 'Haven't you got anything smaller?' Apparently not. I took them but resolved to use my own in-ear set on the day.

The mike was another matter. It was tiny but had some kind of booster that was the size of a Havana cigar and weighed the best part of a kilo. I hadn't lost a load of weight to substitute it with that. Again however there seemed no alternative.

Lee was worried by my concerns and immediately suggested a post-climb interview in the studio instead. I thought it through. I really wanted to make the recording. I love *In Touch* and Radio 4 and valued the opportunity I was being given to broadcast my belief that disability need not be crippling. I'd said on-air that I'd do the diary and ducking the challenge now, on the eve of the climb, felt wrong. And, having had hopes of it being filmed raised and deflated, I rather fancied the idea of a permanent record to refer to in years to come.

I weighed the steel tube in my hand again, measured the length of the wire and made up my mind. 'Okay, it can go in my daypack. I'll take it.'

Lee protested all the way to the steps of Broadcasting House; I reassured her that I'd only be operating the equipment between pitches, when I was securely anchored and my hands and mind would be otherwise unoccupied. Reluctantly she agreed but only after she'd joined the lengthening list of people I'd call the moment I was safely back down.

The very next morning I received an email from Triple Echo, the production company responsible for making *The Adventure Show* for BBC Scotland, apologising that they had not got back to me earlier, assuring me that they were very keen to feature the climb in the series but could not send an entire film crew to Hoy. Instead they proposed shooting an interview either before or after the ascent, taking some long shots from the cliff opposite and interspersing footage taken with a Go-Pro camera – if I'd wear one. What did I think?

After picking my jaw up from the floor I rang Matthew. 'What's not to like?' he asked. I agreed.

After that the news just got better. Margaret at Triple Echo was not exaggerating when she wrote next with the news that she'd 'got a great camera person' to join us on the trip. Keith Partridge is quite possibly the greatest mountaineering and adventure cameraman there is. His CV includes award-winning films like *Touching The Void*, *Alien vs Predator* and ground-breaking documentaries such as *The Edge, Lost Land of The Jaguar, Human Planet* and the jaw-dropping *Beckoning Silence: North Face of The Eiger*. And now he was going to be filming me!!

Having worked with Keith previously, Martin was delighted. He thought that Keith might have been to Hoy before to film Catherine Destival's ascent, which had Matthew scampering off to find footage . . . for reconnaissance purposes of course.

It was with some jubilation that Matthew, Andres and I sat round the dinner table at Matthew's house on the final Thursday before our departure. We had had a last session at Swiss, attacking the seriously overhanging 7a+ route whose final 15 feet run out at 30 degrees off-vertical, and had all nailed it. The gentle warm-down on the bouldering wall had however almost ended in disaster when I'd slipped and trapped the ring finger of my right hand behind a hold. Ice and tape seemed to have reduced the swelling and I could move it again, if a little stiffly. My climbing slippers too had survived and my feet, though rather gnarly after so much abuse, were in good shape.

The three of us were buzzing with excitement – this time next week we should all have stood at the summit of the Old Man of Hoy and be enjoying a few drinks in the local hostelry. We opened a third bottle of red, flopped onto sofas and turned on the DVD player.

First up was *The Big Climb*.

'Fuckin'ell guys this film is so ancient, it's like what the 1940's or something?'

'Watch it pal,' I growled, 'you're sitting next to someone who was alive when this was shot.' I received a thump from Matthew for pointing that out.

Like Kate, Meg and Laura though, their mirth was quelled by the sheer size of the rock and by the time Bonington was edging out of *The Coffin* they too were seeing themselves there.

Next we loaded *The Long Hope*, a film of Dave MacLeod's ascent of Britain's toughest climb, a gruelling 23-pitch, 500-metre E8 6a route on St John's Head which is the highest point on the cliffs that run behind the Old Man. Close-ups of crumbling rock, projectile-vomiting fulmars and vast overhangs left all three of us feeling queasy and glad we were attacking its little brother. The fact that MacLeod and his partner decided to climb the Old Man afterwards, just for kicks, didn't belittle our task, merely put it into context.

I left my two climbing partners surfing the Web in pursuit of Ms Destival and headed home; a bit pissed, a bit trepidatious, a long way from where I had been a year before and on the brink of achieving a lifelong dream with two recently made but already very important friends.

17

Day 1, Journey to Hoy

'Sometimes the best gear for a climb is a good excuse.'

– John Sherman

I'd packed, unpacked, double-checked and repacked at least half-a-dozen times over the weekend. Matthew and I had compared lists, hoarded chocolate and bonk bars and, all the time, kept a wary eye on the weather forecast – which was improving.

Flights had been booked, passports found (Andres panicked when told he needed to produce one, fearing he should have got a visa to leave the country and travel to Scotland!) and, on the basis that our young Colombian friend was a student and therefore highly likely to over-sleep, Matthew had insisted that Andres stay with him the night before we flew. That way he could also check Andres had remembered his harness.

As my house was en-route to the airport, the taxi with the other two in it was due to pick me up just after 7.00 am. Anticipation woke me before the alarm and, unable to go back to sleep I headed downstairs. It felt odd shuffling round the kitchen before Kate or the girls were up and I was halfway down a second cup of coffee and checking the weather forecast on Hoy for the umpteenth time before they appeared.

Never at my most communicative in the mornings, I found myself lost for words and gratefully accepting a piece of toast I didn't really want, to provide my mouth with alternative employment.

A sensitive child, Laura gave me a hug and said, 'Don't worry Dad, whatever happens you'll be the first blind person to attempt the Old Man and I'm proud of you.'

The taxi arrived promptly to take me out of limbo, and final farewells and hugs seemed suddenly all too brief and hurried. Matthew hefted my 70-kilo rucksack into the already groaning boot of the car and stuck me into the passenger seat next to the driver, and then we were off.

Huddled in the back and cradling his iPhone, Andres was moaning that this was no time of day to be awake – or if he had to be he should be heading for bed with a girl. Matthew pulled out his Blackberry and embarked on a stream of client calls that lasted three-quarters of the way to Luton, leaving me to talk vanilla to the driver. Eventually a lull in electronic chatter allowed me to ask what the two of them had got up to the night before at Matthew's house.

'Oh you missed out' Matthew enthused. 'We watched Catherine Destival soloing the Old Man. So much more exciting than watching Bonington or even MacLeod doing it!'

'Yeah, she looked really hot,' sleazed Andres, 'you know, really sexy. You're gonna be such a disappointment for that cameraman after her.'

They carried on waxing lyrical all the way to the airport where I pretty much switched off, allowing myself to become a piece of hand luggage to be processed and fed through the system and into my seat on the plane. At least with Matthew taking responsibility for me this time there was no question of being stuck into a one-size-fits-all-disabled-people wheelchair to satisfy airline Health and Safety legislation. It's rather perverse to be chair-bound when I'm jetting off to climb a rock-face.

Only as the plane was taxiing to the runway, did Andres reveal his fear of flying. I felt suddenly guilty. All the focus had been on getting me aboard; there had been no space for this to come out or opportunity for him to nip off for a quick smoke to quell his nerves. As a former fellow sufferer, I babbled away for the next hour to take his mind off it and fed him Polos to stop his ears popping.

Perhaps the flight landed early, or Martin and Nick were a few minutes late – either way Matthew was getting twitchy by the time they found us in Inverness's tiny arrivals hall. The sun was out and the temperature a few degrees warmer than it had been in London as we trooped across the car park to the minibus that was to be our transport for the next five days.

There we were introduced to Keith Partridge whose crates of camera equipment took up two-thirds of the back of the van. He was about my age, had a South of England accent and an air of calm capability that immediately put me at my ease. As we were also to discover, beneath his affable and highly entertaining good nature he possessed a rugged self-sufficiency that had kept him alive in the most inhospitable environments on the planet.

We loaded up and were on the road within a matter of minutes. As I sat back in the seat between Matthew and Keith I felt the stress slough from me. This was actually going to happen. From now on it was Martin's gig, he'd done this before. All I had to do was climb.

Martin had planned an afternoon's sea cliff climbing at Latheronwheel. As I understood it, to blow away the cobwebs, check I was still in shape and assess the abilities of Matthew and Andres.

As we sped through the Caithness countryside Keith kept us amused with tales from his latest gig – filming a downhill mountain-bike race in the Himalayas from the back of a motorbike, while Andres dozed in the back, propped up by rucksacks and camera paraphernalia.

After about 90 minutes we pulled into a little seaside car park and had a quick bite to eat from the provisions Martin had brought, before loading up with climbing gear and setting out along the cliff-top path. A light drizzle fell but the sun burnt hot behind it so that a heady aroma rose from the heather and flowers that brushed our boots as we trooped in single-file. London's bustle and traffic seemed centuries distant.

Martin found an anchor for the top rope and began to set up. Matthew, who had been bringing up the rear with Andres, approached him and asked what they should do.

Martin seemed surprised. 'Er, there's a couple of VDiffs over there if Andres feels up to leading them.'

I only half took this in. Keith was telling me that he wanted to get some footage showing me in action before Hoy, to give people an idea of the challenges I faced as a blind climber and to introduce the team.

Putting these two conversations together in retrospect makes it perfectly clear what was happening, but the penny only dropped much later, by which time Matthew and Andres had been written out of the picture.

My mind was elsewhere. What I love most about climbing is that it requires total concentration. If you have other things on your mind you'd better shelve them or you're heading for a fall. My blindness becomes merely another problem to be overcome, like the absence of a good hold when you need to pass a bulge – if I let it become an issue I'll never get past it.

The routes I climbed that afternoon were pretty

straightforward, a VDiff and a couple of VS's, all on the kind of rock I love, hard sandstone with juggy holds and good long cracks to wedge fingers and toes into. The cliffs face east so we had the sun at our backs most of the time but idyllic as it was, I was troubled by the occasional flicker of worry. I put it down to caution; after all I hadn't come this far to get injured now.

I guess that's why, when Martin and I had a mix-up, I reacted the way I did. Nick had led the route and Martin was climbing slightly above me. I'd already mentioned I prefer a guide to climb beside and slightly below me, but Martin clearly preferred his way and this seemed also to suit Keith and the camera.

I was resting as he made his next couple of moves. He began by treading on my fingers for the second time that afternoon. I stifled a yelp and shook out the pain. Six feet above he stopped, turned and looked down to me. 'Climb when you're ready.'

I started to feel my way up.

Martin and Nick were of course using the opportunity to reacquaint themselves with climbing with me – it's a head-fuck for most people. At Easter Martin had led most of the routes, leaving Nick (or on the *Cioch Nose*, Alex) to climb with me.

In my mind the guide is there to keep me from straying too far off the route and to locate hand, or more usually foot, holds when I'm beginning to struggle. Martin had a pre-planned route in mind that he wanted me to adhere to – I suppose because he felt that this is what I am used to at the climbing wall. It didn't help that from his perspective my left was his right. At the base of an off-width crack with an awkward little bulge, I asked twice whether he really meant me to move my left foot. It was bearing most of my weight so was the only thing keeping me in balance.

He assured me that wriggling it a couple of inches further out would give me a better position. As I fell my left big toe was wrenched back 90 degrees and I heard him mutter 'no, the other left.'

Trust is a big part of climbing. I snapped, 'It WAS *my* sodding left!' and climbed the remainder of the route in silent fury following *my* instincts. Ten minutes later, sitting on the cliff top massaging my throbbing toe, Matthew and Andres sidled back to ask whether Martin might leave the top rope in place so they could use it. Catching the edge in Matthew's voice and feeling a bit mutinous, I piped up that of course this was their climbing trip too and I was sure we had another rope that we could set up further along the cliff. At that point I would happily have climbed with them instead, but had just agreed to do a final route for the camera.

Keith fancied something a little more dramatic to round off the afternoon's filming and, notwithstanding my toe, so did I. Leaving the rope for Matthew and Andres we set off in search of an HVS described by the (admittedly ancient) guidebook. This section of the cliff was overgrown and proved to be a bit loose in places but something that looked like it might fit the bill, with some steep rock leading up to an overhanging bulge, caught Nick's eye and we abseiled down to its base. With the waves ten feet below spattering us with foam, Martin and I waited as Nick cleaned the route and laid protection. He grunted a bit at the top, disappeared over the bulge then shouted down 'Off belay!' A minute or two later we heard the command 'Climb' and I was off, ahead of Martin this time.

It was a chossy, loose and vegetated climb that got a bit hairy in the final ten to twelve feet especially when the chockstones wedged in the narrow overhanging crack decided to give way under pressure. But I had momentum and was up and over the ledge at the top and grinning stupidly at the camera lens within minutes.

'I reckon that's a new route,' Nick said. 'It's got to be an HVS 5a or b, that bulge was a bit more bold than I expected. I'll check with the SMC but if it is a first ascent what do you want to call it Red?'

It was a nice problem to have on a sunny afternoon. Martin had joined us by now and we tossed names around for a few minutes before settling on *3 Blind Mice*. (Sadly it had been climbed before but gratifyingly had been logged as an E1).

'You certainly motored up that one,' said Keith. He had been pretty quiet up to now. 'The trouble is, Red, and I mean no disrespect here, you climb so fast and make it look so straightforward, that anyone looking at the film won't know that you can't see.'

'Aye, it's difficult to keep pace with him on the rock sometimes,' Martin agreed.

Keith was too amiable for this remark to have been made with any side. He clearly loved his job and went about it with such assuredness that most of the time I'd forgotten he was there.

'I suppose I could use the white stick . . .'

'Or we could get a guide dog,' Matthew, who'd joined us, chipped in acidly.

'Um, no. I was thinking we just need more footage of when it's a struggle to get around. Like with the walk-in over the cliffs.'

'You wait till you see me trying to clamber down the cliffs to the Old Man' I said ruefully 'No one'll be in any doubt then.'

'I'll be short-roping him, in case he takes a tumble,' Martin confirmed.

'Too right, but I'm more worried about turning an ankle or cracking a shin than breaking my neck – especially crossing those boulders on the causeway.'

'I think I'll come down the cliff with you then and get some footage to set the scene.'

It was agreed, as, somehow without my noticing, had been the consensus that Nick should lead all five pitches up the Old Man and Martin climb with me.

Back on the road again, Matthew and Andres simmered with discontent. They'd had a rubbish afternoon's climbing, stuck firmly on the sidelines. Slower on the uptake, I hadn't fully appreciated the ramifications of the latter point, yet.

The bleak outskirts of Scrabster matched the atmosphere inside the minibus as we approached the ferry terminal and it was a relief to get out on deck and feel the sea breeze on the crossing to Stromness.

'Paging Mr Pitt, paging Mr Pitt – the camera needs to love you!' crowed Matthew arriving to lead me to the viewing platform at the stern.

In front of us the shoreline of Hoy glowed as red as coals in the slowly sinking sun, vast and dramatic. Once Matthew had pointed my head in the right direction and I'd followed the line of his arm I saw the Old Man rising proud and erect – a sentinel before his cliffs. Keith shot minute after minute of me in atmospheric contemplation of the scene, but it hardly felt staged. I could have gazed at it for hours.

Martin remarked it was the calmest crossing he'd had in the two dozen or so he'd made and boded well for the weather ahead. I was already convinced – I'd felt the lure of the rocks ahead of me, it was going to be a great climb.

There'd been a fair bit of banter during the crossing; most of it about Matthew and Andres being my entourage and me the Brad Pitt star-figure; and the mood had seemed to lighten. Keith was sensitive to the fact that the three of us had come this far as a team and took the time to explain the need to keep what might only be a 15-minute feature, simple. Too many faces would crowd the picture, the focus had to be on me and my quest.

At Stromness it was a minute's drive to the Ferry Inn where Matthew helped me up to my room and we were finally able to discuss things alone.

He was seriously pissed off, fulminating about Martin all-but ignoring him and Andres at Latheronwheel. 'I can completely understand his reasons for not wanting us all on the Old Man at the same time, though I still think that's more about what suits him best. But I thought that at least today we'd all get to enjoy some time climbing together. Instead he couldn't get rid of us quick enough.'

'I'm sorry, I didn't realise that you were going to be pushed aside all afternoon. I thought Keith only wanted to get a few shots.'

'You know what Red? This is about getting you to the top of the Old Man, that's Martin's job and he's doing it. Of course the rest is secondary. But his attitude sucks.'

I agreed that Martin seemed to be making it perfectly clear that he viewed Matthew and Andres as excess baggage but wondered whether he was wrong-footed by the presence of the camera. After all, though a little taciturn at times, he had been far more accommodating at Easter.

Matthew laughed grimly, 'This is great PR for Martin Moran. He's going to be the man who led the Blind Man of Hoy on TV. The fewer of us in the picture the more screen time he receives.'

'I'm sorry about all this, Matthew. I had no idea it was going to turn out this way,' I said, feeling somehow responsible.

'The only thing that matters here is achieving the right outcome for you. Andres and I will be happy enough knowing that we got you most of the way to the top of the Old Man.'

I muttered something about preferring to have one of them climbing next to me than Martin which Matthew picked up on straightaway and I was soon explaining about the mix-up on the cliff.

'So you're more comfortable with Nick guiding?' Matthew cut straight to the chase as usual. I nodded. 'Well, tell Martin then! This is about optimising conditions for you, not him. His feelings don't matter here.' Suddenly Matthew's gripes had become secondary.

I said I would think it over and we hurried downstairs to join the others in the bar where Martin and Keith outlined the plan for the morrow. The weather forecast was good so we'd catch the first ferry across to Hoy, drop our gear at the hostel and walk straight over to the Old Man. There, on the promontory, Keith proposed using the day to shoot an interview with me.

'It'll just be asking you a few questions about what drew you to climbing in the first place; why The Old Man of Hoy; how you came to choose Martin to lead you up and the impact that losing your sight has had,' he assured me.

'That will give Nick and me the opportunity to take Matt and Andres up the Old Man and Keith can get some pictures of them from the cliffs,' Martin added his stamp of approval to the plan. 'Then we can take you up, Red, the following day if the weather holds, or if not Friday looks like the better day with no rain forecast until the evening.'

I felt a wave of disappointment. It had been bad enough to be told that the three of us weren't going to climb together but somehow I'd always assumed I was going to be first up. The idea of talking to a TV camera about myself while my two climbing companions were behind me, making the ascent I'd dreamed of for thirty years, was galling. Still at least it would give them a day off from what was rapidly turning into *The Red Szell Show* and it meant I could order another beer without compunction.

Everyone loosened up a bit with a couple of drinks and settled down to a jovial dinner during which Keith and Nick took centre stage and told climbing stories. We rounded things off with a dram of whisky and got a relatively early night.

18

Day 2, All Talk, No Action

'The Old Man sticks straight up out of the
Atlantic like the admonishing finger of God'
— Al Alvarez, *Feeding the Rat*

Light framed the Velux blind and I was up, scrubbed,
dressed and packed before I thought to check the time and
found it was only four o'clock. I went back to bed, fully
clothed, alternately dozing and reflecting on the daylight
hours this far north.

Martin had slept in the minibus, having given up his
bed to Keith – there being no more room at the inn for
last-minute additions. I'd clearly woken him slinging my
rucksack into the boot at 7.00 am on the dot but, gazing
across the car park to Scapa Flow, he was happy enough
to chat about the German fleet scuttled there at the end of
World War One.

It was a beautiful summer morning, bright and with a
briskness that made it a pleasure to be up so early. The
previous day's anxieties had no place here. Matthew
and Andres appeared happier too; clearly buzzing at the
prospect of the climb that lay ahead on what looked to be
the perfect day for it. They tucked into bacon and eggs
with gusto then stood hungrily on the ferry deck as we
chugged closer and closer to the Isle of Hoy.

The warden of the hostel lived by a cluster of bothies,

one of which Nick and Amy had rented with friends for New Year's Eve some years before. Their revels had acquired primitive authenticity when they had been plunged into darkness by a power-cut. It looked an inhospitable enough place on Midsummer's Day.

Soon enough though we were rounding the bend into Rackwick Bay and pulling up by a smart stone-built bungalow in front of which the famous sign was propped. Battered, peeling and long detached from its post it still spelt out its stark warning:

OLD MAN OF HOY
CLIMBERS ARE HEREBY WARNED
THAT THERE IS NEITHER
SUITABLE RESCUE EQUIPMENT
NOR EXPERIENCED ROCK
CLIMBERS IN THE VICINITY
CLIMBERS THEREFORE PROCEED
AT THEIR OWN RISK

Martin was keen to get cracking within the hour so I busied myself making sandwiches while the others got their kit together. Keith unloaded boxes and boxes of camera equipment and it soon became clear that everybody was expected to act as Sherpas. I alone was to carry just my own bag, partly so that I could concentrate on making it along the cliff-top path in one piece, partly for on-film continuity.

I pulled a face at this special treatment but, listening to the others grunting and groaning under the additional weight, was secretly glad to be conserving my energy.

The footpath led along spectacularly beautiful coastline so grand in scale and vibrant in its blues, green, white and ochre red sandstone that even my damaged eyes could not fail to take in its magnificence. All around us seabirds wheeled and squawked. Curlews, guillemots, skuas, kittiwakes, puffins and the dreaded fulmars – winged traffic in an avian city, honking and shouting at each other. Occasionally, like the hooter on a Model T Ford, the unmistakeable throaty sound of a corncrake echoed over the moorland, announcing that it wasn't extinct yet.

Though recently rebuilt and about as even and well made as these things get, the path was hard going for me. To be in keeping with its rugged surroundings it was constructed from scree laid in a trench about eight inches deep and had narrow drainage channels cut across it at irregular intervals to twist misplaced ankles. Larger chunks of rock littered the way and its verges just to add extra interest. I've had more difficult walks to a climb but this was still two miles of hard labour and concentration and I was glad I was borrowing Martin's hiking boots again.

After about a mile the path began to descend. 'You should be able to see the top of the Old Man from here,' announced Nick, whose rucksack I was holding onto for guidance. I peered along his arm and made out a rather disappointing block toppling sideways into the horizon.

Only as we walked out along the promontory did the Old Man truly begin to loom. One glance over the edge of the cliff was enough to give anyone pause for thought – it was a dizzyingly long way down.

Still, it looked very climbable and I was horribly jealous as I waved Matthew and Andres goodbye and listened to them jangling away down the precipitous 'path' to the foot of the cliff. Keith suggested I eat something and have a cup of tea while he set up his various cameras, so I found a solidly planted boulder to perch on and took his advice.

Over the next 40 minutes Keith gave me regular

updates on the progress the others were making on their long descent and outlined the interview process. I was to remember that this was a voluntary exercise and I could choose not to discuss any aspect I felt uncomfortable with or ask him to stop filming at any point. This was reassuring, not because I have deep dark secrets I wish to conceal but because being filmed was a new experience for me. In fact the major relief of having this escape option turned out to be that because the day was so bright it hurt my eyes to look too long at the camera and we had to stop for me to take refuge behind dark glasses. I refused to be filmed wearing them though as I have a pathological distrust of people who insist on being interviewed in sunglasses – it's irrational I know but I think it makes them look shifty!

With Martin making rapid progress up to the first belay stance, Keith performed some final adjustments to the camera he had focussed on the Old Man then turned to face me. 'Are you ready then, Red?'

'As I'll ever be I guess.' The breeze had got up and sitting inactive on a headland I'd got chilly in spite of the sun so had put on my Mammut waterproof.

'Mmm,' Keith clearly didn't approve. 'Have you got anything a bit more colourful, black isn't great for these kind of outdoor shots.

I rummaged around in my pack and pulled out the bright yellow down jacket I had, once again, borrowed from Cole.

'Perfect!' Keith was delighted. 'Great colour!'

So much for Mammut sponsorship I thought. I'd make sure to wear their natty little rucksack on the climb.

Andres was following Martin up. Their shouted communication carried to us on the wind. I'd suspected the four of them would split into these pairs. Matthew and Martin were both just too alpha-male, too used to taking the lead to get on well. Andres was Alex's age and Martin treated him as such. And Nick just went with the flow. The strange thing was, the most alpha of all of us, the one who quietly called the shots and you knew would walk out of the jungle after a plane crash, was Keith. But being a natural peacemaker he was content to keep a lower profile.

He got things rolling by asking me to talk about when I'd first started climbing then led into my diagnosis, the prognosis I had been given and what I had had to give up.

'So what led you back to climbing again?'

'As soon as I got back on a wall I felt that sense of freedom that climbing had always given me; even more so. I'm not prodding around with a white stick, I'm actually feeling with my hands and my feet and I'm concentrating completely and utterly on it. Funnily enough I just forget I can't see for a bit.'

With Nick shouting down from the belay for Matthew to follow him up Keith asked me to describe some of the challenges I faced as a blind climber and I began to talk about how Matthew, Andres and I had worked to overcome the obstacles.

Keith stopped filming and said gently, 'I'm afraid we haven't really got time in the feature to introduce lots of other people. For the purposes of the programme Martin and Nick are the ones helping you.'

Too many characters clutter a story – I knew that from writing fiction but could only imagine how disappointed the others would feel at being airbrushed from the narrative. Keith read my thoughts. 'I know they've helped get you here but ultimately this is your story, your challenge. It will have more impact if there are fewer faces around you.'

Martin was now edging across the traverse on the

second pitch; a long drop and big pendulum swing if he fell; he'd have chosen Nick to belay him. At least I'd have the security of being on a double rope here. Any fall I took, would still be a drop and swing, but significantly less hair-raising.

'So give me an assessment of Martin and Nick and why you've chosen to climb the Old Man with them.'

That threw me. I put my hand up and asked for a moment or two to think about the question. Keith obliged and I asked what exactly he meant.

'Well, why climb with them? What kind of characters are they? How do they, and you, work together as a team?'

My mind flitted between Moy, Diabaig and Latheronwheel. The three of us worked well together, alone and in our designated places. I'd climb anything Martin thought I was capable of, so long as he led and Nick was nearby giving his calm directions and prepared to accept that I might not always follow them.

'Well, Martin's the expert. He must have climbed the Old Man more times than anyone else, so I know I'm in safe hands and he'll get me back in one piece. And Nick's so laid-back I'm surprised he doesn't topple backwards off the rock face.' It wasn't the best answer I could have given but I hoped it would suffice.

'So, are you nervous?'

'I am a bit nervous about it but it's a bit like going into a school exam if you've done all the revision then you can only do what you can do on the day. And it's just a waste of energy to worry about what might or might not happen.'

I got the impression that Keith would have appreciated a more tense reply and wanted to press me further but at that point we were joined by a group of walkers from the mainland keen to watch the live show on the rock.

From this distance the climbers appeared like Lego men scaling a battered grandfather clock. We fielded questions about them and I realised that the walkers thought I was Keith's assistant and that we were filming this ascent. It gave me a strange twinge of resentment that was both unworthy and revealing. Was I perhaps beginning to believe that this was *The Red Szell Show* and so guarding the limelight jealously? If so I'd better guard against coming over as a pillock on film.

Keith had a HUGE telephoto lens trained on *The Coffin*. An extremely competent climber himself, he was fully qualified to offer commentary on the technique displayed by others. A series of 'hmnh's, 'ah's and a final appreciative 'well done!' accompanied the regular clicks of the shutter as he caught Andres' exit for posterity.

'That was certainly a bold approach to it,' he remarked to me, 'he's a strong climber.'

I agreed and added that he'd see very different methodology from Matthew. Within the hour my words were borne out.

'He's looking a bit tense in there' Keith relayed, 'would you like a look?'

I'd had a couple of gos at peering down the telephoto lens but the image I got, because it was so hugely magnified and close-up, was just a blur of pixillated colour across my narrow tunnel of vision – impossible to get a fix on. This time however the centre-point was dead-on a readily identifiable object – Matthew's face – and it didn't look happy.

I'd already registered the decrease in chatter wafting across the water towards us and the sight of Matthew's stricken face made me recall something Cole had said a month or so before: 'Red I have no doubt that on the day you will pull it out of the bag. Matthew might be dried pasta; hard until he gets into hot water.'

'Come on Matthew, commit and go for it; you can do it' I urged, leaving the camera to Keith to get some shots that Matthew would either treasure or want to delete.

'He's going for it . . . he's out . . . go on . . . go on . . . yes, he's jammed the crack . . . looking a bit wobbly but . . . no he's okay. Well done!'

A huge relief settled over me. The two of them were practically home and dry now – they'd nailed the crux and could enjoy the climb.

With much of the tension and the walkers gone Keith resumed the interview.

'So, Martin tells me you've said that preparing for this challenge has made you a happier, better person, less likely to dwell on your problems. Would you agree?'

'For a long time I was scared I was going to eat myself up with worry and perhaps a bit of bitterness about my eyesight and I still periodically go and stick my head over the side of the deep well of despair and think "that's a long way down, I'm glad I'm out of that." But I don't know; I think I've lived with losing my eyesight for so long that you realise that the only way to combat it is to come out fighting every day and set yourself new targets.'

'Just how important is it for you to reach the top?'

'It's important that I do get to the top to show that you can't always judge a book by its cover. I do think that for too long people have imagined how awful it would be to have a disability and for many of us the worst part is learning the news the rest is fighting back.'

'What scares you most?'

'What, about the climb or life in general?' I retorted, on my guard for imaginary traps.

'Either.' Keith was un-phased.

I thought. Seconds ticked by. 'Er, not much really.' I supposed I was meant to say 'failure' or 'falling out of the bottom of *The Coffin* and dangling 150 feet above the Atlantic' but really apart from losing my family in some random tragedy there's not much out there to give me sleepless nights. I did my best to explain this, hoping I didn't sound cocky or glib, then asked Keith to stop the camera.

'I'm going to say something that I'd prefer not to be filmed but might give you an idea of why I find that question hard to answer. My mum died a couple of years ago and I gave the eulogy at her funeral. After that nothing else seems so frightening.'

Keith nodded and we took a break to walk along the cliff so that he could recce a possible vantage point for a second camera the following day. Like me he had been a great fan of *Blue Peter* when he was growing up and confided that it had been a proud moment when he'd at last earned a *Blue Peter* badge, for filming the programme's 2008 expedition.

We chatted about the glory days of John Noakes and how we'd followed Chris Bonington's exploits as kids. Keith's first commission as a freelance adventure cameraman had been a documentary in the Himalayas with Sir Chris. 'After delivering the film to the BBC, I was walking back out across the car park wondering what on earth I was going to do next when I bumped into a producer I knew coming the other way. He asked whether I was free to come and work on a programme he was about to start making. That was *The Edge*!' He'd been on a roll ever since.

Back at the promontory I could just make out the helmets that Andres and Matthew were wearing, bright flecks of manmade colour against the ochre rock. They had made short work of the next pitch and were up amongst the nesting seabirds.

'Ah, fulmar-vomit time. I wonder whether any of them have been hit yet,' Keith said with relish and put his eye to the long lens. 'Yup, looks like Nick's been got.'

Feeling more relaxed I settled down for his final few questions which finished with the influence of the Paralympics on raising awareness of disability.

'I think the age of pushing disability under the carpet and hoping it will disappear is over, but the struggle for recognition as equal people goes on,' I opined. 'And if getting to the top of the Old Man can help push the struggle a little bit further into the past, then all well and good.'

Content with the fruits of his labours Keith turned his attention to the others. They were nearing the summit and he began to take photos as first Martin then Andres appeared against the horizon. As quickly as they'd popped up they were gone again to be replaced 20 minutes later by Nick and Matthew.

'What on earth is he doing?' I hadn't thought much could surprise Keith, clearly Matthew could.

'Oh shit, he's not is he? Is he dropping his trousers?'

'Worse, he seems to be stripping down to his Y-fronts.'

'They're not Y-fronts, they're Speedos.'

'Why? Does he do this a lot?'

'Only for charity. Some of the guys he swims with at Highgate Ponds told him they'd double their sponsorship money if he got to the top of the Old Man in his budgie smugglers.'

'He'll want photographic evidence then,' Keith sounded amused and bent his eye to the viewfinder to catch the money shot. I raised my hands overhead and applauded beside him incredulous that Matthew had done it and praying that he was securely anchored.

A couple of minutes later the summit was deserted

again. With Nick and Matthew preparing to ab off, Keith began the lengthy process of packing away his gear. As he did so he told me about filming the Galician percebes gatherers in Spain who, between waves, sprint out into the surf beneath the cliffs to where the largest gooseneck barnacles grow, harvest a few, then sprint back to safety before the next breaker dashes them against the rocks. 'That really is life on the edge,' he said.

Within the hour we'd been rejoined by the others. Matthew and Andres were elated, buzzing with snippets of drama from their ascent; enormous exposure, 'thank god' holds, amazing moves pulled off in the nick of time, loose rock and angry seabirds. They'd been gone slightly less than five hours and returned as Tom Patey once put it: 'a little older in wisdom, a little younger in spirit.'

Keith, though, had a wary eye on the gathering clouds and mindful of the slower pace I kept, suggested he and I made a start back to the hostel while the others de-harnessed and got themselves sorted.

There was plenty of time before supper to relive Andres' amazing E5 move out of *The Coffin* and onto featureless overhanging rock. Generally attested to as being 'very bold' it, like Matthew's nervier exit and countless other memorable moments had been caught for posterity by Keith. All of which could have been very helpful to my own attempt the following day had I only been able to see them properly.

Matthew drew me aside and said he'd had a word with Nick about him and not Martin climbing beside me. Nick was okay so long as Martin agreed. Though I hadn't asked Matthew to, I might have guessed he would. As with the whole project, he simply didn't do *laissez-faire*. Realising that someone needed to set the ball rolling he'd taken it upon himself. Job done, he departed in search of mobile coverage so he could tell his wife about his day, leaving me to talk to Nick and Martin.

Nick was typically laid back. 'I'm fine either way Red. It's up to Martin though.'

I bit the bullet, asked Martin to step outside and began with an apology. 'I'm sorry Martin, this isn't really very easy to say, but if it's all the same with you I'd prefer it if Nick could guide me up the Old Man tomorrow and you lead. It's nothing personal' I continued awkwardly, 'it's just that, I don't know, maybe because we're the same age, or because we both grew up in Sussex and learned to climb at Harrison's, I feel a bit more in sync with Nick. But if that doesn't suit you for some reason, or messes things up, or you feel it's your responsibility to be climbing beside me, just say because I'm only expressing a minor preference.'

There was a long pause. 'I suppose both jobs are of equal importance. I'm happy to lead again.'

A wave of relief that this wasn't going to be an issue came over me and I began to apologise all over again. Martin stopped me; his decision had been made, it was time to move on to supper.

I did my best to join in with Matthew and Andres' celebrations but, for the same reason that I only had a single glass of wine, felt limited by the fact that I had yet to share their triumph. Following the two of them outside later for a cigarette that I didn't really want but at least kept the midges at bay, I discovered that their pleasure was not unalloyed. For some reason Martin had been in a hurry to leave the summit as quickly as possible. He'd forgotten to tell Andres to sign the logbook and insisted they abseil off before Matthew and Nick joined them.

'So we didn't even get a photo of the two of us together up there,' grumbled Matthew.

I shrugged. Suddenly I was very tired and the following day was going to be even longer and more exhausting. I had no energy for this. Stubbing the cigarette out half-smoked, I binned it and said I was going to turn in. On my way to bed I passed Keith showing Nick how to operate the Handycam that he, not Martin, would now be using to film me on the overhang.

19

Day 3, First Ascent of the Old Man by a Blind Man

'At its finest moments climbing allows me to step out of ordinary existence into something extraordinary, stripping me of my sense of self-importance'

– Doug Scott.

Martin wanted us up and ready for 9.00 am. I'd slept well but woken with a gyppy tummy and spent a worrying 15 minutes on the loo hoping to rid myself of whatever hadn't agreed with me, before pulling on the same clothes as the day before (for continuity's sake).

Matthew had made sandwiches for us all and they, as well as a flask of redbush tea and a hunk of the fruitcake Martin's wife had baked for the climb, went into my daypack beside the water, chocolate and bonk bars that had taken up residence there.

It looked to be another perfect day for climbing as we set out along the now familiar path. The previous night's rain had not been heavy and had, according to Martin, stopped in the early hours. Between them the sun and a light wind were well on their way to clearing away any residual dampness, the seabirds wheeled lazily overhead and the corncrake was again in fine voice.

On the promontory my entourage came into its own. Under Keith's careful scrutiny Matthew and Andres busied themselves connecting me to the various pieces of recording equipment I was to carry.

Keith had swathed my climbing helmet in gaffer tape fixing a Go-Pro camera on top and various microphones inside it. Matthew fed the wires down my back and under my harness to Andres who connected them to the tiny MP3 recorder Keith handed him. This was packed into a bum-bag and strapped round my waist. I also had the chunkier Radio 4 machine for the audio-diary. Keith had offered to let me copy the files from his, but he was recording the whole climb and I had no idea how to edit them and knew Lee wouldn't have time to sift through it all, so decided to stick with my original plan.

At last all the levels had been checked and I was pronounced ready to go. A final hug from both Andres and Matthew, words of encouragement, a rope fixing me to Martin and I was off, arms outstretched beside me for balance as I lurched down the steep path towards the pounding surf below.

It was hard slog. The path, such as it was, tacked at a steep angle about 300 feet across the face of the cliff as it dropped the 450 feet to the water's edge. We were in the lee of the promontory and as we worked our way further down and across into the crook of the cliff the air grew humid and heady – almost tropical – from the rich array of seaside plants and flowers. There were even large butterflies flitting around us. Such an abundance of plant life did at least mean there was plenty for me to grab hold of on the many occasions I slipped or stumbled on the loose rocks underfoot.

Keith was getting loads of footage that would leave his viewers in no doubt as to my visual abilities. This was less a scramble than a four-limb crawl and I was streaked with sweat before we were even halfway down.

'If you tell me you need to do another take of that Keith, you'll be pogoing on your tripod!' I gasped between gulps of water, when finally we'd reached the perfect smuggler's cave that lies at the head of the rockfall causeway.

'No, don't worry, it's all good. I'll just go and set up the camera.' He strode away, showing no signs of fatigue despite having spent the last hour running rings around us to catch every angle of my descent while carrying both a large TV camera and a rucksack stuffed with all sorts of other kit.

I recharged my energy levels with Mrs Moran's exceedingly good cake and a Snickers bar.

Nick, it transpired, was to carry my daypack and while Martin clipped a comprehensive range of cams and hexes to his rack, Nick removed all extraneous items (right down to a lip salve and spare roll of tape) from my bag, leaving only food, drink and MP3 recorder. I had just enough time to record a brief entry in my audio-diary, catching the jangle of Martin's protection, the subdued roar of the sea and my breathless awe at the scale of the monolith towering above me, before Martin had us on the move again, scrambling across wardrobe-sized blocks that had once formed a 500-foot high sea-arch.

We were a good 20 feet above sea level and I was all too aware of the water churning below as I clawed my way across the deep crevasses with Martin and Nick watching my every move like hawks.

I made it with only minor cuts and bruises but was glad to flop on a flat block and allow my heart rate to calm as Martin and Nick prepared the ropes and checked the equipment. Keith gave me space until he saw me pull out my climbing shoes when he came over to conduct a quick 'before the off' interview. For the life of me I can't remember what I said. I suspect I tried to convince him that I wasn't that nervous but imagine my wide staring eyes told a different story.

I was finally going to do it. After 30 years of dreaming about it, I was about to climb the Old Man of Hoy! Nervous energy crackled through me. I wasn't scared as such; I knew no great harm should come to me with Martin and Nick there. The fact that Andres had narrowly missed being hit by a falling rock the previous day in some way was reassuring; that one at least wouldn't be coming my way. What else was to come would have to be confronted when it came. For now I just wanted to get started; get some upward momentum and hopefully keep it going for 450 feet.

Keith filmed me squeezing my feet into the battered shoes and then tying into the bright pink rope that Martin and I had decided was the colour I stood the best chance of seeing. A final safety check and Martin was climbing, the protection at his waist tinkling like wind chimes as he rose above us.

Fifteen minutes later and it was my turn. The rock was warm and textured, like the armoured skin of some living prehistoric beast. The first move was a reassuringly easy pull up onto a large block, followed by a step onto a ledge with big holds all the way. I said something like 'Onwards and upwards' in my relief. Only another 444 feet to go, I'd made a good start and was finally on my way.

The route took me off the east and onto the south face, which was bathed in bright sunshine. The heat was a little uncomfortable but the reflection was worse. RP leaves you with very light-sensitive eyes. Sufferers usually get cataracts as a result. If you've had those removed and your eyes, like mine, are blue, any bright light is exceedingly painful. I'd weighed up the pros and cons of wearing sunglasses but decided against, on the grounds of needing all the little vision I could get. Now with the rock glaring into my streaming eyes I was regretting the decision.

Fortunately the pitch was little more than a big blocky staircase so I made rapid progress, only slowing at a particularly loose section where Nick advised me to test every hold before relying on it, and we soon reached the large belay ledge, known as *The Gallery*, where I could tuck myself into the shade of a niche.

Martin checked I'd securely clipped into the belay and was off again, edging round a corner that led down to the traverse onto the east face, one of the Old Man's trickier and most exposed sections.

Nick paid the rope out slowly and with long pauses. Having caught my breath I began to rummage for the MP3 recorder, unsure of how long I might have till I was to follow.

Self-consciously I murmured a ninety-second account of what we'd just done and how I felt, then tailed off. In spite of the sun there was something eerie about the ledge; pieces of kit from long-forgotten climbs, rusted pitons driven too deep into the rock to be removed, karabiners that had long ago lost their shine and were clipped through a dozen frayed nylon slings, no single one of which you'd trust your life to – all destined to remain there until the Old Man toppled into the sea.

The recording was still running, picking up the buffeting wind and the peep-peeping of circling seabirds. I began to speak again:

You might be able to hear the fulmars in the background. Fulmars are 'foul gulls' so-called because when you get close to them they're liable to projectile vomit on you: a horrible, sticky, fishy-smelling goo which they use as self-protection and can project up to two metres apparently. Nick who is belaying Martin at the moment, has just been hit by a fulmar haven't you Nick?'

Yeah, I got shat on actually. At least it's not quite as smelly as the vomit. But exactly the same place as yesterday on the same left side of my shoulder but yesterday was on my back, today it was on my front; not very pleasant. So I'm just matching up; I've got a white splodge front and back on my left shoulder.

If you come back tomorrow you'll get one on your right.

The previous day, Andres had been so freaked by these angry birds (who make a sound like they are being throttled before they regurgitate over you) that he had opted to bypass one pair of them. In an effort to stay out of range, he had wriggled along a narrow horizontal crack beneath the ledge they guarded, and got stuck – much to everyone else's amusement.

Judging by the rope length still coiled at our feet, Martin still had some way to go to the next belay stance so I asked Nick:

What do you have to do different with a blind or partially sighted climber?

I guess talk a lot more. Erm . . . you kind of naturally do stuff with clients and you say 'just look at me, see what I'm doing here' if it's a technical section you kind of explain it to them just by climbing it. But with yourself it's definitely a lot more of having to explain what happens. And it's a good challenge you know it makes you do something that you don't normally do which is to put into words what you're doing physically.

Finally, and a little unfairly, I asked him how he rated my chances of success. There was a long pause.

I'd say, pretty much, I think, 100%. Basically you're going

to do it, there's no two ways about it. I mean if it gets difficult then you'll have a wee rest and then carry on. And you've got the total ability to do it. It's not like you're going to hit a brick wall and say 'I refuse. I can't do this. This is impossible.' You're just going to say 'this is hard. I need a rest. Okay now I'm ready to do it.'

It was precisely what I needed to hear. No platitudes, just a professional review of my abilities with a gentle reminder to quell my tendency to rush at things. If I listened to him and remembered not to try and force the route, I'd be fine.

'You've got an audience,' said Nick as I tucked the MP3 away. 'There's a wee crowd round Matthew, Keith and Andres.' As on cue they began to wave and shout but what they were saying was lost beneath a heavy droning above St John's Head. It filled the sky then passed low overhead, heading out to sea.

'That was a big puffin,' I said to Nick.

'RAF Hercules' he corrected. 'Your own private flypast. He waggled his wings at us too!'

From far above and round the corner we heard a faint, 'Safe!'

'Off belay!' Nick shouted back, feeding through some slack. Then to me, 'Shall I take that bag?' Martin would be ready for us to start behind him in a minute or two.

The crux pitch beckoned – the section that would decide whether I made it to the top or got thrown off this gigantic finger of rock. I had to believe in my own abilities; Nick and Martin did. So did Andres and Matthew – and they'd all shown me it was possible. Two hundred people had sponsored me to a total over £10,000 so far (Matthew had checked that morning). My progress was being followed on-line, by TV and radio. That, more than the long drop below, gave me a chill sense of exposure.

I checked both ropes I was now tied into for a third and final time, took a deep breath of mind-clearing sea air and banished all these thoughts. The red cliffs fringed with sparkling white surf and clear blue sky, the life teeming above and below me and the ancient rock I rested on, all gave me a sense of something infinitely greater than a few personal concerns. I was here solely and simply to enjoy climbing this glorious chunk of sandstone and the best way to do that was one move at a time.

'On belay!'

'Take!'

Martin pulled through the two lines till first pink, then green were taut.

'That's me on pink! That's me on green!' I shouted.

'Climb!'

'Climbing!' I replied and, turning my back to the promontory, felt for the ledge below with my feet. I edged down into a high-sided gully that led me towards the corner between the south and east faces. It was steep and uneven. Nick was close on my heels.

'So you're now on a little pedestal, it's quite a large pedestal. You can move rightwards on it. Shuffle rightwards but not forwards. That's it.'

'Okay, is this where there's a gap?'

'Then there's a gap, yeah.'

'This is where if I could see and looked down, I'd see . . .'

Nick chuckled nervously, 'You wouldn't want to.'

I transferred my right hand to the left, inside, wall and found a jagged flake of rock, about the size of a tea-tray for support as I inched my right foot forward. It found the edge.

'You need to step round the corner and find the ledge on the other wall' Nick said.

'How far?'

'Two, two-and-a-half feet.'

'And 150 feet straight down,' I thought grimly. The Atlantic was churning all too audibly between my feet as I toed the edge of the pedestal.

I tested the flake, it felt solid enough and anyway it was the only decent hold in reach. Edging my hands as far round as I dared, I hung off it and stepped my right foot into the unknown. An inch or two lower than I'd hoped it found a ledge that felt about half an inch wide and was slippery with loose sand but gave enough purchase for me to stretch out my right hand and locate a side pull. I matched feet and was round.

I remembered from *Feeding the Rat* that Al Alvarez had found another narrow ledge at scalp level for his hands and brought my left arm above me in search of it. It too was as dusty as the top of an old picture frame but allowed me to find my balance and catch my breath.

'Well done Red.' Nick had popped his head round the corner. 'If you step down an inch or so, you'll find a wider ledge to stand on. It might be more comfortable.'

It was, till it ran out after about 18 inches, leaving me stretched like a starfish on the traverse. If I slipped now, even double roped as I was, I'd swing a good 20 feet across the face of the rock and into one of its solid buttresses.

'The handhold you've got for your right is the only decent hold there. You need somehow to match both hands on it, match feet too, then step across to the right where you'll find a side-pull at fingertip length. It's a bit of a faith move but there's a ledge for your right foot.'

I followed instructions. The ledge sloped down to the right and I had to rock over onto that leg to stretch far enough for my fingers to locate the side-pull. All the time my left hand was clamped round a hold about the size and texture of half an avocado. Fortunately it was dry and having been used by five pairs of hands in the last 24 hours, clean of debris. The side-pull was much better and I drew myself gratefully across on it to come to rest at a corner underneath the first chimney.

A cheer arose from the promontory and I could hear Nick's grin as he patted me on the back and said, 'Awesome, that's one of the hardest bits.'

We must have descended a good 20 feet from our belay ledge, which always feels somewhat counter-intuitive when you're climbing, so I was happy to be going vertical again, even if the rock was steep and overhanging. Now however I found just how annoying it was to have a Go-Pro fixed to my helmet. That it added a bit of weight and heft had been a little off-putting at first but as I headed upwards I discovered the real trouble of having something the size of a satnav rising proud of the smooth lines of my safety hat.

'Fucking Go-Pro!' I muttered as it caught on yet another piece of overhanging rock and jerked my head back. 'I hope it's well insured.'

'You're certainly testing it to its limit,' Nick agreed.

'Yeah, well I don't reckon anyone will be in any doubt that I can't see if they use any of the footage from it. Assuming it survives.'

But the chimney itself was a delight. Dirty, a little damp and slippery in places but with deep cracks for fingers and toes and wide enough to bridge comfortably.

Near the top Nick asked whether he could pass me so as to help guide me out onto the arête. In doing so he managed to step on my helmet. 'Fucking Go-Pro!' we said in unison bursting into a fit of the giggles.

I found a gorgeous niche hold for my right hand and a little plinth to push up on underfoot and pulled smoothly out round the jutting corner of the overhang and onto the right-hand arête. It was bristling with holds and within a few relatively straightforward moves I'd achieved my reward and was bridging the base of *The Coffin*.

The natural line to follow as you climb this bottomless chimney draws you deeper and deeper into it as the cracks converge at the back of the flue. I knew I needed to head out before I hit the roof at the top; I'd watched Bonington make that mistake and read of Alvarez's struggle to exit; but like them I was reluctant to leave the safety of good holds for the seemingly featureless walls on either side of me; besides there was the most enormous hex to remove from a fist-wide crack above me yet.

All climbers operate on a 'you lose it you replace it' basis and it becomes ingrained – partly out of habit, partly out of pride – that as a second you do your damnedest to remove all protection put up by the lead climber; especially the really expensive pieces.

Nick was now on Jumars so he could film me on the Handycam. He read my thoughts and insisted, 'I'll get that. You concentrate on getting yourself out.'

I'd already gone too high and was tucked up under the roof with my head on one side. The effing Go-Pro kept bumping the rock above me and in my best public school accent I reprised Chris Bonington 'my wretched crash hat is too big'. I should have moved down a few inches but my right hand was in a good ledge and my left had hold of a flake like a scallop shell that would be equally good for my right when it came to it. My feet were the problem. The right was wedged into a horizontal crack and taking most of my weight but try as I might I could find nothing for my left which was jammed against the wall behind me and kept sliding down the sandy surface. I moved my free hand down and hurriedly brushed the sole of my shoe clean, but to little avail.

'You need to come out of the back and swing round onto the left hand wall in a minute.'

Nick was right and the sooner the better. I was getting tired and thoughts of the drop beneath had begun to flit across my mind. Matching hands I hung most of my weight from the scallop-shell hold, braced my leg against the wall behind me and wiggled my foot across it in search of the first reasonable bump it could find. There was nothing. With infinite care and my heart in my mouth I edged back and swapped feet so I could try my right foot instead.

'Down an inch!' Nick sounded tense too as my shoe scraped blindly across the wall behind. 'A little to the right.' My toes bumped over a wrinkle, reversed over it and found the merest edge to hang on. 'Got it!'

Time was of the essence now. Telltale quivers ran through my legs; I had under a minute till I'd have to retreat and rest, or more likely peel off the wall and have to do the overhang on Jumars.

Using ten valuable seconds to get my breathing under control I inched my left hand out and groped round the edge of the overhang for a hold. All I found was blank wall. I tried to get my head out from under The Old Man's belly but the camera wedged, pushing me down: 'Fucking Go-Pro' I howled.

'Out further, an inch maybe. Up a little. That's it!' Nick urged.

My fingers closed on an impossibly smooth nubbin of rock. 'This one?! You've got to be kidding Nick!' I protested.

'No. That's the only one. Palm off it then you've got a crack above right for your other hand.'

My right foot had begun to slip. I pulled back in, hung with aching arms off the scallop, then re-placed it and stretched out for the nubbin again. 'Shit or bust' I muttered and rose into a wobbly Egyptian. On tiptoes now I jammed my right fist into the crack above. Both feet swung free for a sickening moment before my right landed exactly where my left had been while the left slid down the outside wall to an 'oh thank god' ledge.

I shuffled along an inch and brought my right foot round to join its fellow. Heart thumping I caught my breath. I was out! Hopefully the worst was over.

Groping blindly for a better left-handhold met with no success, so I rose up on tiptoes; bad move! My left leg began to jiggle up and down like a sewing machine.

'Handhold, Nick?'

'Up and, er, left. Well . . .'

I couldn't hang around any longer so stood on the nubbin to gain height. It pushed me out left, away from the crack but I'd found a small ledge for my fingers that was enough for both hands. Legs trembling, partly from effort, partly from relief but in the main because my balance was off and my position precarious, I rested for a few uneasy seconds during which I had time to question my sanity.

'That'll work. Awesome. Well done.'

'Straight up or head right?' I demanded.

'Straight up and head to the left a bit.'

The wall above felt blank, and steep. Out at ten o'clock there was a small ledge and I rocked over towards it. From then on it was a bit like progressing up Andres's *Rockover Route*, just hairier and with less margin for error.

'You're doing it yourself, you don't really need me.' But Nick kept me trending left and with a hand-width crack developing in front of me and a series of jutting ledges to my right it became obvious why. Using both I began to build a rhythm and could finally breathe easy again.

'You're over the crux, well done.' The voice from above made me jump. Martin's face peered down at me. 'Everything all right?' he asked.

'Bloody marvellous thanks, Martin' I gasped, dragging myself up past his boots and across the rope. 'Now I see why they call it *The Coffin* – it's bloody difficult to climb out of.'

I'd done it! Jubilant cheering erupted from the promontory but I was so exhausted I couldn't even make out the red mass of the cliffs. I unzipped my pocket and pulled out a squashed and warm bonk drink sachet. It tasted revolting but was like mainlining caffeine. Within a minute I was beaming. Within two I was recording my elation in my audio-diary. Within three Martin was off up the next pitch.

Nick was full of praise: 'You did that really nicely. Well done, Red. I should have some great footage on the Handycam.'

I'd made it to The Haven! Tucked into the niche of what is surely one of Nature's most perfect belay stances I was buzzing as I tried to take in the beautiful panorama spread out ahead of me, the feat I had just achieved on the rock-face below and all the while fighting the urge to laugh for the pure joy of being alive and climbing.

In comparison to what had gone before, the next 80 feet was easy. I needed little guidance from Nick as I tacked first right, then left, to follow the crack-line up the east face. The regular ledges provided secure footholds and only the occasional fulmar – all of whom must have vented their bile on Martin because they left me alone.

Half a dozen moves in, I remembered what Andres had said the night before: – 'I felt in too much of a hurry; I forgot to enjoy the climbing.' I'd done the hard part, I could afford to slow down a little and live the dream.

I am surprised that Channel 4 has not yet featured extreme pissing as reality TV – there's probably a website dedicated to it somewhere though. As far as 'atmospheric and extreme' goes, taking a leak while facing out towards *The Long Hope* route on St John's Head was pretty spectacular. As Nick and I attempted to direct our streams over the fulmars swooping beneath I remarked: 'You know I'd love to go back and have another go at *The Coffin*. I reckon my exit looked pretty ragged. I bet I could do it more stylishly next time.'

Nick laughed. 'Let's get you to the top first. But we can always come back next year if you want.'

The fourth pitch was another 'glorious Diff' and a 120-foot geology lesson rolled into one. My fingers were spoilt for choice amongst the textures and features of the beautifully stratified wall, including arcs of rock-iron that feel as though someone had buried sections of iron drainpipe in the sandstone, and which provide the best side-pulls known to mankind.

The wind had got up and moaned deeply around the corner of the fourth belay ledge. Martin took the Handycam from Nick to film some footage of me topping out.

'You just open it up like this and it starts filming,' Nick demonstrated.

'And that's all I need to do?'

'That's it. Easy.'

The guys on the promontory were waving to us and shouting again, but it was snatched away by the wind so we just waved back.

After Martin had gone Nick and I shared the ledge with a little puffin that landed on the next ledge down with its fish dinner just as I was tucking into my own snack. Nick directed my gaze and after a couple of minutes hard staring I finally made out its sleek black shape perched just a few feet from me.

Its noisy munching made the ledge, which was littered with the debris of previous climbs, less haunting. I had the impression I was high up the buttress of some long-abandoned gothic cathedral about to scuttle beneath the gargoyles and up onto the roof.

Nick described the route ahead: 'It's a big corner, with a crack in the back of it. Do lots of bridging. There's more ledges on the right-hand wall than on the left-hand wall. And at about halfway, so after about ten metres, there's a bit of an overlap, a bulge you go over, but it's pretty straightforward. At that point there's then a crack in the left-hand wall. I'll be behind you so I'll be able to direct your feet but I won't be able to see your hands.'

'Okay.' One last overhang between me and the summit; how appropriate it should end this way.

He gave the dreaded Go-Pros a final once-over. The battery on his had died but mine was still running. I'd made my audio-diary entry while gazing for, and then at, the puffin, then left the recorder running to give a flavour of the climb itself.

'That's us!'

'On belay'.

'So basically it's straight up.'

'Yes.'

'Climb!'

'You go first. I'll just dismantle this belay.'

'Climbing!'

'I'll try and catch you up. The speed you go I'll be lucky.'

'Climbing!'

The story of the fifth and final pitch is the one I shall take from my library to tell myself during winter nights of the soul when I am consumed by self-doubt or rancour.

There were lots of handholds spread across the dihedral wall. I tend to talk to myself as I climb anyway so there was no difficulty thinking of things to say into the mike clipped to my collar:

This is lovely, lovely rock. Big cracks and ledges to get your hands and feet jammed into. It beats the climbing wall any day and I sat within sniffing distance of a puffin. What a day!

Nick was clinking along behind me, shouting the odd direction but in the main leaving me to it.

I'm now leaning right out 450 feet above the Atlantic . . . er . . . searching for a handhold . . . arrgh . . . got it! All I can say is that if I didn't have RP I would probably never have done this . . . so . . .

There's a couple of bits of gear above you . . .

Scrape, crunch, heavy breathing.

The gear's right in front of you now. About to hit your helmet.

Clunk.

Climb up the left hand side of it.

Left? Okay. So come out of this corner a bit.

Most of the holds are on the left hand wall.

Is there anything for the left foot?

No. Good right foot, nothing much for your left foot. Er, you've just taken your foot off the foothold. Right foot down. You can actually . . .

Ah!! I've got a lovely foothold here.

A bit of grunting and scraping, the sound of protection snagging me, then:

Bastard!

Behind your head and above your head; on the right-hand wall. Yeah, just there.

You might have to come out of the corner a bit for it. Just move your hand around. That's it. Well done! If you want to pass the gear to me.

Krak . . . runch!

Day 3, First Ascent of the Old Man by a Blind Man

Ah just taken the Go-Pro out. Excellent!

I'm coming out over a bulge that bulges out about two feet. So my legs are about 2 feet in front of me underneath the bulge, my upper body is leaning out . . . Got hold of something with one hand and with the other. Ah, the end is nearly in sight. Well it would be if I could see it. Urgh, and over . . .

Here my bold manoeuvre must have dislodged the microphone jack because the recording quality turns to mush. The bulbous section pushed me back and out over the sea, leaving me fist and knee-jamming the corner crack and flailing for both a hand and foothold on my left. Palming the wall I quickly found a jug to pull on, smeared with my shoe and mantled up over the top.

A gust of wind buffeted my face and bright sunshine blinded me completely.

For a moment I thought I must have hit the summit and called out to Martin. His reply came from a good ten feet above. Then it dawned on me – this was the cleft at the top of the Old Man; an eight inch wide split running 20 feet down, as if some giant had taken an axe to the sea stack and tried to split it in two. My eyes slowly adjusted to the glare. The contrast between light and shade; matt red and glittering blue; between shelter and exposure was so elemental and beautiful that I had to stop and catch my feelings.

A final tussle with a troublesome cam and I joined Martin on the ledge just below the summit.

'That's a bit of a treat when you get to the top isn't it,' I remarked about the cleft.

'That's a nice pitch, very positive,' replied Martin.

'I am a truly happy man. I know I'm not quite standing on the top yet. But wow, that's amazing.'

'You're nearly there. You're actually safer than you were a second ago too' said Martin, screwing shut the second of two karabiners securing me to the belay and to him.

'So I'm just going to go onto the top and get some sort of a belay then bring you up. It's only five metres to the top now. We have to be demonstrative apparently,' Martin sounded amused.

'So, first blind man on top of the Old Man of Hoy,' Nick had his phone out and was filming. 'How does it feel?'

'Absolutely bloody marvellous. Dreams do come true. I am so happy! Thanks Nick.'

'Awesome. So, we're just at the final anchor. Martin's about five metres above us. He'll give us a shout in a moment and we'll bomb on up, wave our arms in celebration'

'Excellent. Stand there, have our photos taken for posterity, sign the book'.

'Then bugger off out of here.'

'The pub doesn't open till tomorrow. Oh well, not everything on Hoy can be perfect.'

A shout and a tug on my rope and I was scrambling over the shattered rocks and stunted grass that somehow clings to the top of the Old Man. I fought rising exultation, knowing that when you let your concentration lapse is when accidents most often happen on rock. Nick too was taking no chances.

'Follow my voice. So, you need to cross the gap.'

My fingers measured the distance between the two halves of the Old Man. 'Blimey, it's quite a gap. Blind Man falls between two halves of Old Man of Hoy. That would make for a bit of jeopardy on the film, wouldn't it? Helicopter winches blind man out.'

No one watching me reach the summit would be in any doubt of my inability to see. I crawled on all fours towards Nick's voice, unable to stand. For hours now I had trusted the motion of my body to all of my limbs equally, to sacrifice half of them now made no sense.

'This way,' Nick guided, 'follow the edge then there's a big block about a metre away here for your hand and a flat one next to it you can stand up on.'

'Hey, at last!' Martin called across.

With a supreme effort I stood tall, raised my arms and shouted. 'Yay! I've done it! Thirty years in the making: Yes!' And heard a ripple of embarrassed laughter.

I knew what had happened – and I couldn't care less.

For the first time in the four hours since I'd left the promontory I'd headed off in the wrong direction, unsteady on my legs, in danger of toppling over in the wind, grinning from ear to ear.

'Aye, you know you're on the top of something,' said Martin, coming over to shake my hand.

'So if you just turn round to face the camera and we'll spread out a bit,' he directed.

'Step left a bit, Red. You've got about half a metre.' Nick was still on guard.

With arms aloft we celebrated our achievement, Martin in the middle like some rock god flanked by his axeman and bassist.

'YES!' I bellowed. Then more quietly, 'one of the better days of my life.'

Once he was satisfied Keith had enough footage Martin said. 'So what you've got to do is just nip over and sign the visitor's book and then you can drop down to the abseil before we get hypothermic.'

The visitor's book was an old Woolworths-type notebook stored in a Tupperware box that also contained a Scottish £5 note and a malt loaf, both of which I left for someone hungrier than me.

Instead I scribbled *'Red Szell – first blind man to climb The Old Man'* and the date – *20th June 2012*.

As long as you've climbed the Old Man using a

60-metre length of rope you can descend in three abseils, so avoiding the need to leave a guide rope to re-cross the traverse on the crux pitch. Those who miss the guide rope or have tried to descend in three on a 50-metre length, end up dangling in mid-air beneath the overhang, waiting to be rescued.

Martin was shivering as I slid down the broken rocks to the final belay and keen for Nick to clip on and get going. I'd had a couple of refresher masterclasses at Swiss with Andres' flatmate and fellow instructor Dan, but ab'ing down a climbing wall and down a rock face (especially one as weather-beaten as the Old Man) are about as dissimilar as track-cycling and mountain-biking. I tried blind mountain-biking once – it was a bruising experience.

'I don't know how you don't bash your knees all the time, you're amazing' said Martin, having watched me down the first abseil. I assured him it was just a matter of time and sure enough halfway down the next descent it happened. I was traversing right to left down towards the niche above the overhang, negotiating a succession of ledges and trying not to lose my feet in the deep cracks when an angry squawking erupted between my legs.

I recoiled in surprise, lost my footing as I tried to avoid stepping on the fulmar, spun left on the rope and crashed into a protruding flake of rock. The sharp end punched between two ribs, winding me and provoking a stream of invective against the surprised gull. As the initial shock subsided the pain radiated across my left side. I desperately wanted to test the area with my fingers but knew I had to keep both hands on the rope. Nick, who had seen me arc round into the rocks, guided me slowly down to the niche and asked if I was okay.

'Nothing broken' I confirmed, massaging round the

spot, 'but I'm going to have a bruise the size of a Crème Egg tomorrow.'

Martin arrived and, keen not to dwell on the subject, I asked: 'So we're not going to have another crack at the crux then?'

'You can stop on the abseil and have a feel around,' he replied dryly.

'I might just stick my fingers up at it and go. I've ticked that box.'

'Exactly, you don't need to do it again,' Nick chipped in.

'Yeah, I'll come back when I'm 93, do it as a sort of fiftieth anniversary. You'll still be running the tour won't you, Martin?'

He groaned. 'I'll be going for the oldest.'

'The oldest man on the Old Man.' Nick considered, 'they might film it.'

With no obstacles to negotiate, a 200ft abseil in mid-air is great fun, as long as you're not going first and wanting a dry landing. Nick, who is larger and heavier than me, got blown over the sea and had to swing himself back onto the causeway. But, certain of landing beside him on terra firma, I came flying down the same rope and could not resist a loud 'Wheeee!' as I did so. I was glad I'd followed Martin's advice and invested in a pair of leather rigger's gloves (that Matthew rudely referred to as my 'gardening gloves') – the belay plate was too hot to handle afterwards.

I hardly noticed my throbbing feet as I eased off my climbing shoes. They had survived, just, though my left big toe bulged against the thinned leather.

'I'll sleep well tonight,' I predicted.

Fortified by a large wedge of Mrs Moran's chocolate cake, we started what seemed an interminable slog back up the cliff.

Keith captured my exhausted return for the show and Matthew and Andres were allowed in for a group hug and backslapping session before I collapsed on the grass and, at last, removed my harness. I felt oddly weightless, as if floating in a bubble a couple of inches off the ground; self-contained and detached.

I was dimly aware of a strained conversation between Keith and Nick.

'How did you find using the Handycam?'

'Yeah fine. I think I got some good footage on the overhang.'

'Can I have a look?' Long pause, Keith exhaling in frustration. 'I can't find any files, Nick.'

'They should be there.'

'Take me through exactly how you went about filming.'

'Well, like you told me. I opened the camera up, pointed it in the right direction so Red was in shot and filmed. Then closed it up to stop it.'

'Did you press 'record'?'

Another long silence. 'I didn't think you had to.'

'Clearly.'

'Oh!'

'Shit!'

'What about the Go-Pros?'

'Too wobbly. Only good for short clips.'

'Ah . . .'

A sombre, foreboding atmosphere hung over us on the walk back to Rackwick, reflected in the dark, pregnant clouds scudding low over the bay. We hurried along the cliff path and I think the others would have run had I not been there.

Matthew had already texted news of my success to Omri, who'd posted it on Facebook and before we lost the signal he gave me his phone for a quick call to Kate, informing her of my continuing existence. I didn't tell her everything – there wasn't time.

'Keith went mental when he heard Nick tell Martin all he had to do was open and point the Handycam' said Matthew. 'He ripped off his headphones and started railing.' We'd fallen behind; the rest of the party was out of earshot. 'We tried to tell you'.

'Oh, that's what all the shouting was about. We couldn't hear a word, the wind was too strong.'

'Maybe if you'd been carrying the radios we could have told you via the spare.'

Martin had been against taking them up with us on the grounds of weight and necessity. Keith hadn't been keen either, concerned about crackly radio communication interfering with his audio recording. Besides, Nick was climbing so close I'd had little trouble hearing him. No one had foreseen where they could have proved their worth.

'The thing is, Red, it's all there apart from the close-ups of you on the overhang. The interview, the footage on the boat over, the walk in, all the long shots of the climb are all brilliant. In fact there's probably enough to justify two 15-minute features on the show. But without the close-up footage it loses that edge-of-the- seat feeling and I'm not sure we'll be able to use it at all.'

I'd sensed this was coming. Had he heard me say I'd like to give *The Coffin* another shot? Whatever, it proved you should be careful what you wish for.

'You want me to do it again.'

'Would you?'

We were about to eat supper, a bottle of wine had just been uncorked and if we were going to celebrate it would start now. But the mood was wrong; the shadow of unfinished business was squatting in the hostel with us.

'I'll need to run it past Matthew and Andres.'

'It would only be the first two pitches,' said Keith hopefully.

'Well if they can find something else to do, I'm up for it.'

'It's your gig, Red. If you're happy doing it again and it's necessary for the show then there's no question.' Matthew too must have seen this coming. Not fancying *The Long Hope* he and Andres got out the guidebook and began looking for other places to climb on the island.

Martin, for whom this would be the third ascent he'd led in as many days, had been savouring the prospect of dropping in on the Orkney's folk festival the next day but showed his professionalism and agreed.

Nick merely shrugged and said, 'sure.'

'Okay Keith, I'll do it. But in return can you do me a favour?'

'Name it.'

'Can I have a copy of your audio recording of me doing the final pitch? I pulled the jack out of the machine the BBC lent me.'

With a mutual sense of having saved each other's bacon we settled down to a sober evening contemplating all things climbing – apart from the sea stack two miles up the coast and the rain gusting against the window.

20

Day 4, Take Two

'If there's only one thing I would like to say, this is: enjoy the process. Don't worry about the result. Climbing must be fun.'

– Marc LeMenestrel

Despite being exhausted I slept fitfully. My side hurt and woke me every time I rolled onto it. Andres was snoring in the bunk opposite. And I kept replaying the crux pitch in my head, wondering how I could do it better, if indeed it would be dry enough to attempt, and what would happen if my original success should prove to have been no more than a lucky one-off. Dosed up with ibuprofen I'd finally fallen into a heavy slumber just as the first rays of light were poking past the curtain and I was contemplating getting up to watch the dawn.

'Rise and shine. It's stopped raining.' Martin had the air of a sergeant-major rousing his raw recruits. It was 9.00 am. He'd let us sleep in because it had still been chucking it down at seven when he'd first woken.

'Oh fuck,' moaned Andres, pulling the duvet over his head and turning to face the wall.

I rolled reluctantly out of bed and started to pull on yesterday's stinking clothes – because continuity demanded it.

Nick handed me a cup of black coffee and Martin gave

me the option of melon with my muesli and one or two eggs on toast. It had pissed down till about 7.30 am but now with a light wind and the sun threatening to show its face the rock should be drying off sufficiently. The forecast was clear until about 3.00 pm so if we got a move on we should be okay.

Matthew emerged to wish me luck, then disappeared back to bed with a cup of tea.

It was a subdued trudge across the cliffs. We were four men on the way to work. The muggy weather made my clothes feel all the more rank. I thought of Andres and Matthew. They had the keys to Martin's minibus, sketchy descriptions of a couple of unpromising and rarely-climbed gullies and instructions from Martin to find the off-licence for what we all hoped would be a belated celebration this evening. Whatever happened I had the guilty suspicion that my last day on Hoy would be more entertaining than theirs.

The scramble down the cliff and across the causeway was even more gruelling than the previous day, and it was slippery. I was both mentally and physically shattered by the time I stood at the base of the stack. Keith had set up a tripod near the cave and was planning to use that and a portable camera to get a couple of additional angles. He gave my Go-Pro and MP3 a final check, thanked me for agreeing to repeat the climb, and clambered away to start filming.

Martin began his slow rhythmic ascent and Nick and I got chatting about how becoming a father is like discovering you have an upstairs room in the bungalow you inhabit but that losing a parent leads you to mothball a part of your dwelling space.

The rock was cold and damp, the cracks slick with wet sand that had been washed through the porous stone by the night's heavy rain. At least I had no problem with the glare today; the sun was fighting a losing battle with the cloud. I made swift progress up the first 70 feet to *The Gallery*, feeling looser and better balanced with every move. I could do this, I'd already proved that, but it would be a whole lot easier to repeat the exercise if I was relaxed and in tune with the rock.

'Nice climbing,' said Martin, 'very fluid.'

Before he left he tugged at an ancient and frayed rope that stretched out across the traverse and had acted as a guide back to *The Gallery* for those equipped with 50-metre ropes.

'I'm wondering if I should just cut this down, Nick. What do you think?'

'It's pretty tatty but I suppose it might save someone a cold night someday.'

'Well, I wouldn't put any trust in it,' Martin sniffed, but left it in place.

Without the distraction of making an audio-diary I had plenty of time to consider the crux pitch ahead. As Martin had disappeared round the corner onto the East Face he'd paused to call back 'It's extremely slippery today Nick, you'll need to be careful.' This didn't sound great.

The tea-tray sized flake that had felt so solid yesterday when I used it to swing round the corner and over the two-foot void today felt like half-dried clay, liable to crumble in my hand as soon as I put any pressure on it. It held but tested my nerve.

The east face was like a skating rink. Being in the lee of the wind the sand that had been washed through had settled and built up on every available surface. It stuck to fingers and shoes like grease making every hold doubly hard to grasp. All the friction moves I'd managed yesterday were going to be useless, today would be all about accuracy and balance.

I crept along the narrow ledge, lifting my feet regularly to kick off the sand. The single handhold was smooth as an apple-skin and I tried to dig my fingers into it for extra purchase. My heart was in my mouth when I finally made it to the bottom of the corner chimney.

'That was hairy,' I said to Nick, 'a bit more difficult than yesterday.'

The chimney was filthy and wet, but at least the cracks were wide and jagged, so knowing I wasn't going to be climbing the next day I threw caution to the wind and jammed hands, knees, elbows and feet deep into them with little care for the consequences to my skin. Remembering a technique favoured by Joe Brown, I also put a handful of pebbles in my pocket to wedge into narrow cracks and act as chock-stones, or instant holds, if need be in *The Coffin*.

The walls of that bottomless hellhole chimney were coated in thick, wet slime. At no time while I was in there did I feel anything less than precariously balanced and for once I was in no doubt of my level of exposure. To make matters worse, the big hex that Martin had inserted at the top of the crack had become twisted and stuck.

Nick read my discomfort and swung in on his Jumars. 'I'll try and get that out,' he said 'you feel around for some good footholds. There's a crack behind your left elbow, feel along that.'

It took Nick a good few minutes and the help of a nut key to dig the hex out. He slid it down the rope to me and I attempted one-handed to loop the long sling it was attached to over my head and clip it to the back of my harness with the rest of my gear. It was impossible, I had to let it hang like some bling necklace slung by my navel. I had however found what had eluded me yesterday, a five-toe sized pocket for my foot on the back wall. I scooped as much sand out of it as I could, hung my right in it then edged my left along a jagged crack in the wall ahead. Using the scallop shell hold as a side-pull I could now reach further round the corner onto the outside wall, but my questing fingers still found nothing positive to grip.

'Down a bit. There! That's your handhold.'

'That's it!'

'Yeah, just that sloping one there. When you've stood round and shimmied along the ledge it gets better.'

All the time I was teetering on the edge of balance with the disconcerting feeling that my feet were on molten wax that was oozing down the sides of the chimney. My heart thundered in my ears. Nick was filming, Keith was filming and I was in imminent danger of slithering off this dank wall, plunging down and swinging out to be left dangling in mid-air like a bedraggled spider.

'Good, hang in there. So you can move out onto the left-hand wall in a minute.

Adrenalin pumped round my body. This was it! I had to go now. Kicking my foot deeper into the sandy wall behind me and ramming my fist deep into the crack above my head, I began to lever myself up and out. I flung out my left hand and groped for the greasy slope, willing my aching muscles to defy the pull of gravity for a few more seconds. My right foot started to slip; my heart was pounding.

'Need a foothold for my left,' I gasped.

'Yeah, there isn't any, unfortunately,' Nick's voice was infuriatingly calm.

With a heave I dragged myself round the corner and flagged my left leg as far out as I could to reach the ledge he'd mentioned.

'Up, up for your foot, up, tiny bit, up an inch, left a bit, left two inches. No, the other way. Yes! Well done, Red. That's brilliant, absolutely awesome!'

Breathing hard I hugged the rock and slowly, carefully brought my right foot out to join my left. I was lower down than yesterday with a lot of unrelentingly steep rock to cross till I reached the comfort of the bigger ledges – and I was knackered.

I forced my right arm up and deeper into the off-width crack, ignoring the tearing skin. With an almighty grunt I levered up again, smearing the sloper to reach a pinch with my left hand. Martin had the rope taut, pulling me away from the wall but I dared not call for slack, fearing any jolt would throw me off what little balance I had. I needed to get up, reach somewhere I could rest.

'Handhold?'

'Up and ... you're doing great, you're doing great. Just take a deep breath.' Nick read my discomfort and his soothing voice reminded me to take a break and stop fighting the rock.

'Good. Hang in there, Red. Your left foot can go up and left. Downward. Yes! Nice one.'

With a better leg to stand on I tried to move up again only to find my right shoulder was jammed in the crack. I cursed and yanked it down and out, knowing as I did that it would throw me off balance. Only my fingers straining to hold the pinch stopped me from barn-dooming but once free I was able to throw my right arm high overhead to explore the crack.

'Come on, just one nice little handhold,' I implored, then 'ah that'll do as a handhold, finally!' My hand wrapped around a flat, solid chockstone that didn't feel like it was going anywhere and supported my whole weight as I pulled gratefully up.

It wasn't a chockstone but the large wooden wedge driven in by Rusty Baillie on the first ascent in 1966 and used subsequently by both Chris Bonington and Al Alvarez to aid their climbs. With heritage like that I had no compunction about using it again and patted it gratefully before I matched foot to hand and pushed on.

I lay-backed the crack for a few moves till Nick called, 'Go sideways instead of up,' and I realised that I was heading up underneath the sequence of overhanging ledges. The wall to the left was even more featureless than I remembered and made no easier by the protection slung round my neck.

With each move I could feel my energy ebbing away. My climbing had no fluidity and I knew I was forcing my way up, but I was tired and had only The Haven 25 feet above in mind. I should have stopped and rested but I was genuinely afraid I might not be able to restart. Anyway, I didn't feel in balance enough to be comfortable anywhere.

At last I drew level with Martin's boots and with a final heave mantled onto the ledge. All the cams, slings and hexes snagged at once, checking my progress and leaving me prostrate at his feet. Swearing, I yanked them free and began to present them to him one-by-one. It was inelegant and hardly triumphant but I suppose it reflected the effort I'd put in.

'I'm knackered,' I groaned. 'Just stick me in a corner and tie me to a rock.' But I wasn't there long. Martin and Nick set up the abseil in record-quick time and I was soon pulling on my 'gardening gloves' and preparing for another rapid descent.

The wind was getting up and the sky out to sea looking ominously dark. As I pushed off the top of the overhang I swung or was blown off to the left. Knowing that was the right general direction and that I was unlikely to encounter any sharp obstacles I carried on paying out the rope and dreaming of the foaming pint I'd be enjoying in the not too distant future. A sharp cry from below yanked me from my reverie. 'Go right! Go right! Rope!'

Instinctively I arrested my descent. My left leg had been hooked by something and I was tipping over to the right.

'Rope, Red. Rope.'

I was astride the ragged traverse rope. Mindful of Al Alvarez's experience I had, fortunately, made sure to tighten my harness before the abseil but it was a timely reminder that most climbing accidents occur on the way back from the summit when your mind has already gone to the pub.

Back at the cave Keith was ebullient. 'That was brilliant, Red, really tense. It had me on edge and I knew you could do it.'

'That's a relief, coz I'm buggered if I'm doing it again.'

We were a far happier party for our return to Rackwick. The sun even made a brief appearance, much to the obvious delight of the corncrake.

Though the minibus was there, Matthew and Andres were not, so I had our room to myself. I took the opportunity to get all my gear out, bury my stinking kit deep in my rucksack and then repack everything else in anticipation of an early and hung-over start the next morning. Finding a chockstone still in my pocket I slipped it into the bag as a souvenir. On my way to the shower I gave Martin back the boots he'd lent me, before hogging the bathroom for half an hour and allowing the hot water to massage my aching body.

In the meantime Matthew and Andres had returned, keen for a swim in the sea. Feeling clean for the first time all day I declined the offer but said I'd walk down with them. They hadn't made it to the off-licence so I gave

Martin £40 and asked him to buy some beers and a bottle of whisky.

The others had, predictably, had a crap day. They had gone in search of and eventually located the area mentioned in the guidebook. Its warning about 'loose, fridge-sized blocks' had at least been accurate but to describe the overgrown and tumbledown cliff that they'd found as 'climbable' was apparently highly optimistic. They'd done a bit of bouldering and Matthew had explained the difference between goolies and gullies to Andres but otherwise they'd just mooched about. Their swim in the cold Atlantic was a high point!

With supper and beer on the table and Keith delighted with the day's filming we could finally all unwind. Nick stuck the radio on and to a slew of hits from the past 30 years we tucked in and chilled out.

The show, *Get It On,* was asking listeners to text in requests for songs or artists with one-word names, saying why the song should be played and what they were up to while listening.

'Come on Red, give it a go. I'll text for you,' Nick urged.

'Okay. Erm. Oasis – *Wonderwall.* Enjoying an Orkney ale having just become the first blind man to climb the wonderwall that is the Old Man of Hoy.'

A few beers later and there was time on the show for one last song. And sure enough, with the congratulations of BBC Radio Scotland, I heard my news and it finally sank in.

21

Touchdown

'I look at climbing not so much as standing on the top as seeing the other side. There are always other horizons in front of you, other horizons to go beyond and that's what I like about climbing.'

— Chris Bonington

I was glad I'd had the foresight to pack. We'd paid a visit to the Hoy Tavern, a Nissen hut affair, open two nights a week only and full of good beer and fine locals. Then had a dram or three of whisky at the hostel to ensure profound sleep. If I felt rough the following morning the weather looked even worse. There'd be no climbing today, so we headed for the ferry and home.

On the road Keith kept us going with tales from his time on Siula Grande filming *Touching the Void* with director Kevin Macdonald, including exactly how they created and caught the look of pure terror on actor Brendan Mackey's face in the scene where the rope is cut.

In Stromness he turned to me and said 'You know I spent a lot of time with Erik Weihenmayer when we were filming *Blindsight*. That journey up Lhakpa Ri with those six blind teenagers taught all of us a lot about ourselves and others. It was the most emotional film I've ever worked on. You climb as well as he does.'

Coming from Keith this was high praise indeed. He produced one final rabbit from the hat on the ferry back to Scrabster while he was copying his photos of Andres, Matthew and me climbing to Matthew's laptop as a gift to the three of us. A couple, impressed by his stunning pictures of The Old Man of Hoy, asked whether they could buy one and have him email it to them. Keith told them about my ascent and asked them to leave a donation on my JustGiving page instead. They did, exceedingly generously.

Near John o'Groats we watched a stream of cyclists getting flayed by the rain as they set off for Land's End. 'The things people do for charity,' I mused.

Inverness was dripping when Martin dropped us in front of the same guesthouse I'd stayed at back in April. We shook hands and he presented me with the boots I'd been using as a memento of our adventure.

'I'll use them to get to the Old Man of Stoer with you next year,' I said, thanking him for everything.

He, Nick and Keith all had homes to go to. Matthew, Andres and I had 16 hours before our flight and a Saturday night on the town to kick the arse out of.

There was plenty to keep me busy back in London, starting with an interview for BBC Radio Scotland first thing on Monday morning. As soon as I put the phone down to them it was off to Broadcasting House to deliver my audio-diary to a very relieved Lee Kumutat, in time for her to edit and include it, hot off the press, in Tuesday evening's programme.

The BMC, UK Climbing, *Grough, The Ham & High* and *Scotland Outdoors* magazine had all requested written accounts of the climb and I spent the next fortnight happily retelling the story. The *Ham & High* article was picked up by ITN and for the first time in my life I found myself entering a TV studio.

I was appearing on *London Tonight*, as the feature after the main story about cuts to NHS services at The Whittington Hospital. Local MP Emily Thornberry was there to speak about that and we chatted while we waited to be called through, which helped take my mind off the task ahead. Like me she had gone to school in Guildford and like Nick had stayed in one of those bothies on Hoy. I assured her that I found the idea of appearing on live TV far more nerve-racking than climbing the Old Man, and once she'd completed her interview she came to find me and wish me luck.

Soon after I was fitted with a mike, led through to the studio, introduced to Lucrezia Millarini, then the countdown began and Lucrezia introduced me:

'One of the toughest challenges for any serious climber, contender for the title of Britain's toughest summit, it's a stack in the Orkney islands called the Old Man of Hoy and it's just under 450 feet high. The first successful climb took three days and didn't happen until 1966, 13 years after the conquest of Everest. As I said a challenge for any serious climber, which is why my next guest took it on. Red Szell from Hampstead was determined to conquer the Old Man of Hoy and he didn't let the fact that he's blind get in the way.'

Pia's film of me began to play and I barely had time to feel incredibly flattered by the build-up I'd just received before I was answering questions about how difficult the ascent had been, how and where I'd trained, what level of vision I was down to and how I'd come to lose it. Five minutes flew by and while I wouldn't say I ever felt truly relaxed I found I was really enjoying myself.

'So you've achieved this now, what's next for you?' Lucrezia continued in her easy-going, encouraging style.

I'll carry on climbing. I quite fancy having a bash at the

210

Old Man of Stoer, which is another sea stack but involves swimming out to it. Maybe next year.'

'Goodness me. Okay, well, when you do please come back and talk to us and tell us about that.'

And it was all over. Lucrezia was shaking my hand again and saying, 'I mean it, do come back and well done.'

I was whisked away past David Suchet and Mary Nightingale, thanked for coming in and placed in a cab home, where Megan and Laura had been watching my performance.

They and the flurry of emails and texts I received were in agreement; I had come across well, hadn't appeared to take myself too seriously and hadn't let my nervousness show. Of course I only had their word for it and had to wait for the repeat at 10.30 pm after the national news.

Kate and I sat side by side on the sofa, through the Whittington story, our anticipation growing. The moment came and – the story had changed. A resident of Preston Road had discovered a pony grazing in his back garden. It was a cute little horse and a great story and as Kate said, far more suitable for the dead donkey slot.

There was even better news towards the end of the week when Steve Bate reached the summit of El Capitan. He had had an epic; fate had seemed to conspire against him and Andy all the way, but he had not given in and, though at the limits of his endurance, had succeeded in becoming the first blind person to solo-climb *Zodiac* – one of El Cap's toughest routes. He sounded exhausted but exhilarated as we exchanged congratulations over the phone. Between us we felt we'd stuck two fingers up at the limits RP, and Health & Safety, try to shackle us with.

As Piers Plowright had written on receiving the news from Hoy 'a terrific achievement both for you and humanity.'

Cole, Dan and the other instructors gave Matthew and me quite a reception when we arrived at Swiss for our regular Thursday afternoon session. But Andres was determined that we should not rest on our laurels. Martin had let him lead the final pitch on the Old Man and then suggested on the way back to Inverness that my next step should be to get confident leading on easier routes.

Matthew took to it immediately, while I was more tentative. But for improving strength and technique, Martin's advice was spot on. Also it gave me a new goal to focus on and a reason to keep up with the daily exercise routine.

Lead climbing was however only one of the new challenges that arose as a consequence of the Hoy adventure. Out of the blue I got a call from Jimena, a wonderful instructor at Swiss who had taught Megan and Laura to climb and been my regular teacher after Trevor and before Andres. She was now a manager at Ellis Brigham, the mountain sports emporium. How would I like to learn to ice climb on their in-store ice wall as their way of saying congratulations?

Kate teased me relentlessly. Had I not always said that winter climbing was just not for me? I hated snow and ice, pooh-poohed skiing. But with the sun baking the streets of London during one of the most glorious summers on record, I headed down to Covent Garden to give it a go.

The ice wall is an enormous, two-storey high, 12-foot-square freezer, covered floor to ceiling with thick, lava streams of ice. Dominating one wall and not for the faint of heart, is a jutting shelf overhang.

Jimena helped me into the thermal gear, ice boots and crampons, showed me how to kick my toes into the ice and wrist-flick the ice axes, 'like throwing a dart at a board'. And then I was off.

It's quite different to rock climbing; much less reliant on

hand work and far more about forming a balanced apex on the legs with the ice axes overhead more as a brake than support. After months of being reminded to 'use your legs not your arms' I got the hang pretty quickly and found I could easily identify the difference in sound the axes and crampons made when they had a good or bad bite in the ice. In short I loved it! With ten minutes of my hour to go and blood dripping from my top lip where a shard of ice had crept in under the visor, Jimena asked what I wanted to try for my final route.

'I'll probably come off, but can I have a go at the overhang,' I asked.

I doubt Chris Bonington or Tom Patey would have given me many points for style but with my record on overhangs I wasn't too keen on being slow and graceful. When I rang the bell at the top I knew I was hooked.

I had another chilly appointment to keep. Matthew had, after all, stripped to his Speedos and donned his East German Ladies Swimming Team cap when atop the Old Man and several members of the EGLST had promptly doubled their sponsorship money. In a moment of gushing gratitude I had promised to join them one Saturday morning for a dip in the cold waters of Highgate Men's Bathing Pond.

'Right. You *will* get seriously cold. So bring a thermos of tea, a woollen hat and Cole's down jacket if you've still got it. Otherwise a warm fleece and layers to wear after you get out. Sometimes I'm still shivering half an hour afterwards.'

'You're really not selling this Matthew. I'm getting a bit worried about cardiac arrest.'

'Brain freeze is more likely, but it's been known.'

A group of a dozen men of varying shapes and sizes with matching white rubber caps emblazoned with the

DDR flag and the slogan 'Moob Rule Since 2011' was gathered on the pontoon. The water temperature was, I was assured, a balmy 17 degrees C and the two lifeguards on duty looked in no hurry to come to my aid. I took the plunge.

It was beautiful. The water had a cold bite but was fresh and soft. The surroundings, as anyone who has watched the opening scene of the 2011 film of *Tinker Tailor Soldier Spy* knows, idyllic.

I swam two 330-metre circuits of breaststroke, surrounded on all sides by the others who cheerfully shouted out directions for me to avoid buoys, the perimeter rope and the occasional swan. 'Hey, it's like being on Presidential protection detail,' remarked one American wag.

I got out shivering but utterly invigorated. Every part of my body felt alive and buzzed with sensation. I dressed quickly, glad of Matthew's advice and savoured the tea and the moment as I was made an honorary member and presented with my own EGLST cap. For the rest of the day I was infused with a glorious calm and clarity, as when I've climbed well.

22

What Goes Up . . .

'Getting to the top is optional. Getting down is mandatory.'

– Ed Viesturs, *No Shortcuts to the Top:
Climbing the World's 14 Highest Peaks*

I must have been about five; Mum was pregnant with my sister and probably had her feet up. I was in the garden, up the highest tree I could find – it seemed like a giant but was probably under 15 feet tall. Having summited I had inched my way down and was preparing for the final traverse, along a bough to the pedal car I'd tipped on its side to access the lower branches.

Then for some reason I decided to stop and hang upside down on the bough from the backs of my knees.

Arguably the blood had already rushed to my head before I discovered that this made me dizzy and that I couldn't pull myself back to sitting. I hung there, yelling for Mum, increasingly desperate as the ground loomed then receded before my eyes. At that moment I realised that what people called a fear of heights was actually a terror of falling.

My jelly legs slid their grip and I hit the lawn head first with a sickening crunch. Mum scooped me up a minute later. I was bawling and indignant. Why hadn't she come when I'd called?

Eventually I was pacified with a Walnut Whip. As she

215

checked for signs of concussion Mum explained that she'd thought my shouting was part of a game.

'If you're going to climb things you've got to remember there might not always be someone to help. You need to plan how you're going to get back down again and not do anything silly.'

Though it had started well enough the period following my return from Hoy demonstrated a distinct lack of descent management, with predictably messy results.

The fall came in the middle of a glorious summer of boozy parties. I was spending more time reliving the climb than actually climbing, knocking back a couple more drinks each time I retold the story, then feeling too groggy the next day to do much training.

It all came to a head one night surrounded by other parents from school (again) and began with a mojito that turned into a litre. It culminated with some destructive dancing and someone passing me a spliff . . . after which Matthew and another dad from school had to pour me into a car and take me home. Kate had long since preceded me, feeling under par and no doubt fed up with hearing the same story told for the umpteenth time.

I woke up with a headache and the crushing sense of having let myself down. Just when people were celebrating my success in climbing so high and telling me what an inspiration I was, I had yet again hit the self-destruct button.

An email from Matthew, subject 'the hard man of Hoy' bore testament to this:

now i know what you mean when you talk about 'kicking the arse out of the weekend'
it's brutal and as usual I struggle to keep up with you.
in the meanwhile I guess our next session is still good on Thursday?

Worse was to come. The spectre that had always lurked in the background, of an earlier blind ascent of the Old Man, seemed to materialise a few days later. The email I received was from an individual who claimed to have done so in 1978 and, like me, to have RP. I congratulated him and for a day or two took the news in my stride. Although he could produce no evidence, he then began contacting all the organisations and magazines that had published articles or reported the news of my climb, telling them they must set the record straight. Suddenly it seemed as if my whole effort, which after all had started only as a personal challenge, was being negated; the achievement poisoned.

I got in touch with Keith and Margaret at Triple Echo, to warn them that they may need to amend the script for *The Adventure Show*. Keith wrote straight back to tell me that 'this shouldn't take away from your achievement in my mind!'

Andres was more scathing. 'Just ignore it, man. It's just some sad fucking troll who's got nothing better to do that make up stories.'

'Yeah, now that you're a star you've got to learn to live with these weirdoes. You've probably got a stalker too,' added Matthew.

'What about groupies?' I asked hopefully.

'We are your groupies, pal.'

Another email from this individual suggesting we might meet seemed to confirm Andres' opinion, as did inconsistencies in the dates and descriptions he sent to various websites and people. Finally, he posted a message saying he had been registered as partially sighted when he made his ascent – which as someone else replied is very different to being blind. My claim stood but the experience left me battered and bruised and wondering exactly what the nature of my achievement was.

I began to write about it, as the best way of processing the information. Recalling where I had been and what I had gained put things in perspective. Whether or not my expedition to the summit of the Old Man was a first; other achievements stood unchallenged by anything but my own behaviour. My personal ascent, from an unhealthy rut to a physical and mental peak, better relationships with those I love and strong new friendships, particularly with Matthew, meant far more than a footnote in the record books.

I eased up on my celebrations and made sure that I kept up with my *Cole Styron Fitness Programme* and weekly sessions at Swiss. This however was not enough to keep my newly reinvigorated rat well fed. Because it was school summer holidays my duties as a househusband precluded me from getting away on another climbing trip. I needed to find something that gave me the same physical freedom and sense of wellbeing.

So I became an EGLST regular and have found in its characterful ranks much the same humanity and camaraderie as exists in the climbing community. I still emerge from the water shivering but have bought Cole's bright yellow down jacket from him in the hope that it will help me survive the colder months. Maybe I'll wear it on an outdoor winter climb soon too.

As I've written this account one thing has become abundantly clear to me. When I face a vertical wall of problems or an overhanging bulge of grief and frustration my instinct is to try and get over it as quickly as possible, to fight the wall and flail blindly about for something to haul myself up on. If I take my time to search out the route and break the wall into pitches, I am more likely to remain in balance and rise above it. When, inevitably, the falls and setbacks do occur, far better to be relaxed and in a state to resume the climb out of the shadows. Repeated blind frustration invariably results either in self-loathing or resentment of others . . . or both. Either way it eats at you from the inside.

Though some climbers appear to do it solo, there is always support behind them somewhere. Without Matthew, the Old Man of Hoy would still be my pipe-dream. He, like Mo Anthoine, provided the selfless dedication and meticulous planning that got me to the summit and back, only to become an unsung hero, cut out of the picture in the media coverage.

Neither he nor Andres feature in *The Adventure Show* film aired early that autumn. I hope this book goes some way to setting the record straight.

'You're in so much of a better place than you were this time last year,' he told me at the beginning of October. 'God, you were a miserable git, skulking into Swiss, really angry with the world, moaning, 'I hate this time of year because they put the bloody clocks back' and then going off on some rant about Scottish farmers and the First World War. You're a changed man.'

'I still have my moments' I assured him. But he was right. I wasn't exactly looking forward to losing an hour's daylight at school pick-up time but it wasn't filling me with its customary dread. I walked taller, felt fitter and healthier and more equal to the world than any time since my diagnosis at 19. And that was in no small part down to him.

'How would you fancy coming out to Sardinia and doing a spot of sport climbing? I've been looking at a guidebook and there look to be some great bolted routes out there.'

'That would be great! Yes please.'

'Well, I thought you'd like something to look forward to at this time of year.'

I was speechless. The weather had begun to turn and I'd assumed the climbing season was over for the year. I knew he had a place over there that they rented as a holiday home but . . . 'Yeah, sure, thanks.'

'I thought you might like a little sunshine to look forward to before the long nights set in. I'll ask Andres too. You can fly direct and cheap to Cagliari from Stansted. I'm going to be out there anyway organising a mountain biking holiday for some guys so after that we can have some fun exploring the routes.'

'Thanks Matthew.'

'My job in life is to make you as happy as possible without actually touching you. That's Kate's job.' He replied.

So it was that a couple of weeks later Matthew and Andres met me at Cagliari Airport. I was in high spirits. Total donations to my JustGiving page had just topped £15,000; I'd left London in a cold thunderstorm and arrived to 26 degrees C and bright sunshine.

Andres too was in bullish mood. Unencumbered by childcare duties he had flown out a few days before to recce the local rock.

'You're going to have such a great time,' he enthused. 'We found some amazing routes for you to climb.'

He unfortunately was not sticking around, having decided to make the most of his visa and head off to Brussels for the weekend in the hope of getting his Queen's jewels polished by an ex-girlfriend. (He returned, sceptre tucked between his legs, on the day of my departure.)

But he and Matthew had certainly done their homework and I was glad I'd kept in shape – Matthew was taking no prisoners.

Having waved Andres off, we spent the first afternoon warming up on a nearby crag before heading down to

Castello dell'Iride which is described by Planetmountain. com as:

'one of the most popular crags in southern Sardinia, and now offers more than 60 routes of all grades with a magnificent view onto the Masua sea. The crag faces SE and is comprised of a vertical, sharp whiteish yellow limestone. Many of the newer routes require a 70m rope and plenty of quickdraws. Route names are written on the base of the crag.'

It failed to mention that the area was populated almost entirely by young Polish women in short shorts and bikini tops, tackling only routes graded 6c and above. This was one area of climbing where my failing eyesight was clearly a major disadvantage. I told Matthew of a quote I had seen years before taken from a Cosmopolitan article:

'When a woman hunts for a partner, she is instinctively looking for one who would provide her with a good strong gene pool . . . If he has a tendency to hang from cliffs by his fingertips . . . it's a pretty safe bet he's fit and healthy.'

He snorted. We'd been setting up to climb a 6a called *Down By Law*; 25 metres of sheer white limestone, virtually featureless in places with a fat blocky overhand two-thirds of the way up. As Matthew made a tentative start a young German couple came over to watch.

Skitter, scrape, smack, 'Shit!'

'Ja. I fell off in exactly the same place und made the same noise too,' said the young man approvingly. This did not improve Matthew's mood.

'How old do you reckon he was?' I asked after lowering Matthew back down from his very fluid and successful conquest of the route 20 minutes later. The couple had departed shortly after Matthew had solved the problem the youngster had been unable to pass.

'Dunno, but his girlfriend was gorgeous.'

'Probably doesn't think so much of him now,' I assured him.

Half an hour later I too was descending with a broad grin on my face, to be greeted by Matthew bellowing, 'So Mr. Szell, another optimal result. How sick do you think young Fritz would feel to know he's been outclimbed by two guys twice his age, one of whom is blind!'

'It's all in the genes you know,' I yelled back.

Appendix A

Glossary of some of the more commonly used rock climbing terms

Abseil/Ab – to self-belay down a rope; also known as a rappel.

Aid climbing – (as opposed to free climbing) in which the climber relies on artificial aids inserted into the rock to support his weight. Mostly used on otherwise inaccessible routes.

Anchor – the arrangement of as many items of protection as possible to make the belayer or the top rope secure so preventing them from being dragged from the stance should the climber fall.

Approach – the journey to the base of a crag or route; also known as the walk-in.

Arête – a narrow, vertical ridge of rock.

Arm bar – technique in which the forearm is jammed into a wide crack in the rock to give stability and support.

Ascent – a completed climb.

Barn door – when the body swings out away from the wall because all the holds are on one side, leaving you hanging from one hand and one foot like an open door. Difficult to recover from and often the precursor to a fall.

Belaying – the process of manually paying out the rope to the lead climber, or taking-in rope for the second, while he or she climbs, so minimizing the extent of a fall. The rope is fed through a metal **belay device** attached to the belayer's harness that, in conjunction with a karabiner, creates friction on the rope. The belayer keeps firm grip on the dead rope (slack), close to the belay device, at all times to act as a brake in the event of a fall.

Bolt – a solid metal shaft ¼–½ inch thick with a clip hole for a karabiner at one end, fixed permanently into a hole drilled in the rock to act as protection (typically on sport routes but controversially sometimes as anchors on trad climbs).

Booty – gear left behind by a previous party (usually because they backed or fell off) and is ripe for the taking. Also known as Crag Swag.

Bouldering – un-roped route climbing on large outdoor boulders or problems set on indoor walls, usually to a height of no more than about ten feet. In either case it pays to have a crash mat and a partner 'spotting' for you (i.e. standing at your back ready to break any fall).

Bridging – technique that involves splaying your legs across a gap to create pressure on two opposing holds or walls; also known as stemming.

Bucket – a big, easy-to-grip, in-cut handhold.

Buildering – practicing your climbing skills on manmade structures.

Bulge – a small rounded overhang.

Buttress – a rock formation that juts out from the main face.

Cam – shorthand for Spring Loaded Camming Device (SLCD), a portable, removable form of protection with a trigger mechanism that draws closed opposing serrated lobes allowing it to be fitted into an aperture. When the trigger is released the lobes splay and hold the device firmly in place.

Chalk – usually applied in powder form to keep a climber's hands dry and grippy. Sometimes referred to as 'white courage' and kept close at hand in a stiff-rimmed dip bag clipped to the harness.

Chicken wing – a technique for climbing wide cracks in which you place your palm on one side and brace your shoulder against the other, creating a friction hold.

Chimney – a cleft in the rock face with parallel sides more than shoulder-width apart.

Chockstone – a piece of rock that has become immovably wedged in a crack and may be used as a hold or to thread a sling behind for protection. Some climbers carry small stones with them to place as chockstones.

Choss – loose material on a route: soil, stones, rotten rock, vegetation etc; adj: chossy.

Clean – i) to remove all loose material from a route making it safe to climb; ii) to remove all gear placed by the lead climber (the job of the last person in a party to ascend the route): iii) to complete a climb without falling or resting on the rope.

Clipping – attaching a karabiner to a bolt, rope, or piece of protection.

Clove hitch – a knot often used to tie a rope to a karabiner.

Cow's tail – a short sling tied to the harness attachment point with a lark's foot knot and used in conjunction with a Karabiner to clip into protection allowing you to take a rest.

Crack – a split or fissure in the rock face. Depending on how wide they are bigger cracks are classed as off-width or chimneys. Horizontal cracks are known as breaks.

Crag – a rock outcrop with climbing routes on it.

Crag Swag – See 'Booty'.

Crampon – a grid of metal spikes strapped to the sole of a climbing boot to provide grip on snow or ice.

Crimp – a small hold you can only grip with your fingertips.

Crux – the most difficult move or section of the climb.

Dead rope – the slack section of the rope on the far side of the belay device to the climber, on which the belayer must keep a firm brake hand at all times, preventing it from running-out in the event of a fall. The **live rope** is the section between the belay device and the climber.

Dihedral – a concave corner formation in the rock.

Disco leg – the uncontrollable shaking you get in one or both legs when the muscles are tired and you are on very tenuous footholds. Also known as 'sewing machine leg' or 'doing an Elvis'.

Dogging – short for hang-dogging. The, often significant, amount of time spent hanging in your harness while you try and fail to conquer a route at the limit of your paygrade. Because of its association with unconventional spectator sport, the term is increasingly being replaced by Yo-Yoing.

Drop knee – see **Egyptian**.

Dyno – short for dynamic move; one that requires a jump to reach the next hold.

Edge – a small, horizontal hold or thin ledge.

Egyptian – a technique for extend your reach sideways, achieved by turning your body side-on to the wall, rotating one knee inwards and dropping it as low as you can while bracing your other leg on a good foothold in front of you, thus enabling your outside arm to reach further away from you. From the ground the climber looks like the flying Egyptians in ancient hieroglyphs.

Elevator door – a technique for climbing cracks in which, with thumbs pointing down you pull on either side of the crack as if trying to force a pair of lift doors apart.

Epic – an ordinary climb gone dangerously wrong either through bad weather, injury and/or poor planning.

Exposure – the bowel-loosening sense of it being a very long way down if you fall.

Figure 8 knot – the most common way of tying the rope to the climber's harness.

Finger jam – often painful and bloody way of obtaining purchase in cracks too narrow to fit your hand into.

Fist jam – wedging your fist into a crack to obtain purchase.

Fixed protection – gear that is left on the wall for future use (eg: bolts).

Flagging – method of extending your arm reach on one side by sticking your leg out on the opposite side to act as a counterbalance; helps prevent barn-dooring.

Flake – a rock formation where a thin slab of rock stands proud from the wall enabling you to slide your fingers or a sling behind it.

Free climbing – climbing without relying on artificial aids or fixed protection to support your weight. The rope and any protection you place is there only to catch you should you fall.

Free soloing – to free climb with neither rope nor protection – risky!

Frenchies – pull-up exercise designed to develop lock-off strength, that involve holding your bodyweight on arms bent variously at 45, 90 or 130 degrees.

Friend – a popular brand of **SLCD**.

Gaston – a hand grip in which the thumb points down and the elbow faces outwards enabling you to press sideways against a hold for support.

Grade – the approximate measure of technical difficulty of a climb or route.

Hand jam – using your hand to gain purchase in a crack

by twisting, bunching or spreading it across the width, often employing the oppositional force of the thumb. If the rock is jagged, the hand often emerges looking like it has been smeared with jam.

Hanging belay – a belay stance where there is no ledge to stand on, leaving the belayer is suspended in mid-air from the anchor on the rock face.

Harness – a thick nylon webbing belt with thigh loops and a system of buckles to secure it tight to the wearer. Both climber and belayer tie the rope to an attachment point at the front of their harness that is designed to withstand the impact of and keep them upright in the event of a fall. The harness is also fitted with several belt loops from which to hang gear during a climb.

Heel hook – a high leg technique in which you use your heel to pull down on a hold like a third arm.

Hex/Hexcentric – a hexagonal metal protection device, cast in various sizes, attached to a Karabiner by a wire cable. Inserted into the top of a fluted crack or behind a flake it forms a wedge.

Hold – any feature that affords the climber some purchase for hands or feet.

Incut – an indent big enough to be used as a hold.

Jamming – wedging all or part of your body into a crack.

Jug – i) noun: a nice, big handhold. A jug ladder is a route with a preponderance of such features; – ii) verb: (slang) to Jumar.

Jumar – a type of mechanical rope ascender consisting of a handle and a one-way ratchet that allows the device to be slid up the rope but clamps it as soon as downward pressure is applied.

Karabiner/Carabiner – oblong metal snap-ring with a spring-loaded gate that is used to attach everything to anything in climbing.

Knee bar – wedging your lower leg across a crack to hold you in place, often to give your arms a rest.

Laybacking – technique used in climbing vertical (or steeply sloping) cracks, flakes and outside corners. Gripping the edge of the feature with both hands and leaning back away from it on straight arms you press your feet into the wall beneath your arms and use the pressure created to walk hands and feet upwards.

Lead – to be the first in a party to climb a route, placing and / or clipping into protection as you take the rope up with you.

Lock-off – a one-arm power grip with the elbow closed, that pulls you close into the wall, freeing your other hand to search for holds, place protection or clip in.

Mantle – to push down on a hold or ledge with one or both palms and gain height.

Match – to place both hands, both feet, or one of each, on the same hold at the same time.

Nubbin – a tiny protrusion that may be used as a tenuous hand or foothold.

Nut – a flared metal wedge connected by a wire cable to a karabiner and inserted into a crack as protection. Originally nuts and bolts purloined from the automotive, rail and mining industries, today's custom-made nuts and hexes likewise come in a variety of shapes and sizes for use in different situations.

Off-width – a crack that is neither wide enough to fit the whole body into (a chimney) nor narrow enough to fist jam.

Overhang – a feature that juts out from the wall at an angle significantly beyond vertical.

Pendulum – to swing in a downwards arc at the end of a rope, either because of a fall when the protection above is far to one side of the climber, or deliberately to gain a feature to which no traverse is possible.

Peg – see piton.

Pinch – a narrow hold that can only be gripped by making a pinch with thumb and fingers.

Pitch – a section of a longer climb, generally measured as a rope-length (30m – 50m) or the distance between two convenient belay stances.

Piton – a flat or angled metal blade with a clipping hole for a karabiner, hammered into cracks for protection or aid.

Pocket – a small indented feature, good for a couple of fingers or the tip of your shoe.

Problem – a bouldering route.

Protection – gear placed on a climb through which the live rope is run to prevent the climber from falling too far. Unlike active protection (cams), passive protection (hexes, nuts, pitons) has no moving parts; both types are designed to be removed from a route, unlike fixed protection (bolts).

Prusik knot – a friction knot tied with a sturdy nylon cord that is wrapped round a rope and, like a Jumar, can be slid up the rope as a climbing aid but will lock in place when downward pressure is exerted. Also used as a back-up safety device on an abseil.

Pumped – the swollen, achy feeling you get in your forearms when they are so full of lactic acid that you are unable to grip hold of anything.

Quickdraw – two karabiners connected by a nylon sling, used to link an item of protection to the live rope.

Rack – the set of protection used for a climb, clipped to loops on the lead climber's harness.

Rockover – a complex but hugely satisfying technique especially useful for climbing slabs with few and tiny holds. Involves transferring your weight over one raised knee (often flagging the opposite leg) then rising up to standing to reach a previously out-of-range handhold.

Roof – a horizontal overhang.

Runout – the length of rope trailed by the lead climber before he's clipped into the next piece of protection. Double it to work out how far he'll fall!

Screamer – a long and vocal fall.

Second – climber responsible for belaying the lead, the second then cleans the route of gear as he follows on.

Sidepull – a hold that works best when you pull sideways towards it.

Slab – any rock face or wall on the relaxed side of vertical.

Sling – a loop of nylon webbing, sold in various lengths.

Sloper – a downward sloping hold, often difficult to get purchase on.

Smearing – using friction alone to move your feet up the wall.

Sport climbing – places more of an emphasis on technical ability and strength than trad climbing, usually on shorter routes with fixed protection. As well as bolted crags it encompasses indoor walls and is well suited to competitions.

Stopper knot – tied around the rope above the main (usually figure 8) knot to secure and tidy the loose end.

Tat – old gear, such as slings, karabiners, pitons and rope, left behind from previous climbs. Always advisable to test these vigorously before relying on them.

Thrutching – to wriggle and lever oneself up by any means possible.

Top roping – climbing using a rope that runs through a fixed anchor point at the summit of a route.

Trad(itional) climbing – has an emphasis on longer routes, placing and removing your own protection and the thrill of self-reliance. Also known as adventure climbing.

Traverse – i) to move sideways along a route; ii) section of a climb that can only be tackled by a horizontal course.

Undercling/Undercut – a hold that can only be grasped from underneath, requiring a palm-up grip rather than the more usual palm-down.

Wall – any rock face or climbing wall.

Wire – slang for nut.

Zipper – a sub-optimal fall in which poorly placed protection is ripped out sequentially; often associated with a screamer.